Transportation Law: Passenger Rights and Responsibilities

by

Margaret C. Jasper

Oceana's Legal Almanac Series:
Law for the Layperson

Oceana®

NEW YORK

OXFORD

UNIVERSITY PRESS

Oxford University Press, Inc., publishes works that further Oxford University's objective of excellence in research, scholarship, and education.

Copyright © 2009 by Oxford University Press, Inc.
Published by Oxford University Press, Inc.
198 Madison Avenue, New York, New York 10016

Oxford is a registered trademark of Oxford University Press
Oceana is a registered trademark of Oxford University Press, Inc.

Library of Congress Cataloging-in-Publication Data

Jasper, Margaret C.
    Transportation law : passenger rights and responsibilities / by Margaret C. Jasper.
        p. cm. — (Oceana's legal almanac series : law for the layperson)
    Includes bibliographical references.
    ISBN 978-0-19-537809-2 (hardback : alk. paper)
    1. Transportation—Law and legislation—United States. I. Title.
    KF2179.J37 2009
    343.7309'3—dc22   2008047620

Note to Readers:

This publication is designed to provide accurate and authoritative information in regard to the subject matter covered. It is based upon sources believed to be accurate and reliable and is intended to be current as of the time it was written. It is sold with the understanding that the publisher is not engaged in rendering legal, accounting, or other professional services. If legal advice or other expert assistance is required, the services of a competent professional person should be sought. Also, to confirm that the information has not been affected or changed by recent developments, traditional legal research techniques should be used, including checking primary sources where appropriate.

(Based on the Declaration of Principles jointly adopted by a Committee of the American Bar Association and a Committee of Publishers and Associations.)

You may order this or any other Oxford University Press publication by visiting the Oxford University Press website at www.oup.com

To My Husband Chris

Your love and support

are my motivation and inspiration

To My Sons, Michael, Nick and Chris

-and-

In memory of my son, Jimmy

Table of Contents

CHAPTER 6:
CRUISE SHIPS

APPENDICES

ABOUT THE AUTHOR

MARGARET C. JASPER is an attorney engaged in the general practice of law in South Salem, New York, concentrating in the areas of personal injury and entertainment law. Ms. Jasper holds a Juris Doctor degree from Pace University School of Law, White Plains, New York, is a member of the New York and Connecticut bars, and is certified to practice before the United States District Courts for the Southern and Eastern Districts of New York, the United States Court of Appeals for the Second Circuit, and the United States Supreme Court.

Ms. Jasper has been appointed to the law guardian panel for the Family Court of the State of New York, is a member of a number of professional organizations and associations, and is a New York State licensed real estate broker operating as Jasper Real Estate, in South Salem, New York.

Margaret Jasper maintains a website at http://www.JasperLawOffice.com.

In 2004, Ms. Jasper successfully argued a case before the New York Court of Appeals, which gives mothers of babies who are stillborn due to medical negligence the right to bring a legal action and recover emotional distress damages. This successful appeal overturned a 26-year old New York case precedent, which previously prevented mothers of stillborn babies to sue their negligent medical providers.

Ms. Jasper is the author and general editor of the following legal almanacs:

AIDS Law (3d Ed.)

The Americans with Disabilities Act (2d Ed.)

Animal Rights Law (2d Ed.)

Auto Leasing

Bankruptcy Law for the Individual Debtor

Banks and their Customers (3d Ed.)

Becoming a Citizen

Buying and Selling Your Home

Commercial Law

Consumer Rights Law

Co-ops and Condominiums: Your Rights and Obligations As An Owner

Credit Cards and the Law (2d Ed.)

Custodial Rights

Dealing with Debt

Dictionary of Selected Legal Terms (2d Ed.)

Drunk Driving Law

DWI, DUI and the Law

Education Law

Elder Law (2d Ed.)

Employee Rights in the Workplace (2d Ed.)

Employment Discrimination Under Title VII (2d Ed.)

Environmental Law (2d Ed.)

Estate Planning

Everyday Legal Forms

Executors and Personal Representatives: Rights and Responsibilities

Guardianship, Conservatorship and the Law

Harassment in the Workplace

Health Care and Your Rights Under the Law

Health Care Directives

Hiring Household Help and Contractors: Your Obligations Under the Law

Home Mortgage Law Primer (2d Ed.)

Hospital Liability Law (2d Ed.)

How To Change Your Name

How To Form an LLC

How To Protect Your Challenged Child

How To Start Your Own Business

Identity Theft and How To Protect Yourself

Individual Bankruptcy and Restructuring (2d Ed.)

Injured on the Job: Employee Rights, Worker's Compensation and Disability

Insurance Law

International Adoption

Juvenile Justice and Children's Law (2d Ed.)

Labor Law (2d Ed.)

Landlord-Tenant Law

Law for the Small Business Owner (2d Ed.)

The Law of Adoption

The Law of Attachment and Garnishment (2d Ed.)

The Law of Buying and Selling (2d Ed.)

The Law of Capital Punishment (2d Ed.)

The Law of Child Custody

The Law of Contracts

The Law of Copyright (2d Ed.)

The Law of Debt Collection (2d Ed.)

The Law of Alternative Dispute Resolution (2d Ed.)

The Law of Immigration (2d Ed.)

The Law of Libel and Slander

The Law of Medical Malpractice (2d Ed.)

The Law of No-Fault Insurance (2d Ed.)

The Law of Obscenity and Pornography (2d Ed.)

The Law of Patents

The Law of Personal Injury (2d Ed.)

The Law of Premises Liability (2d Ed.)

The Law of Product Liability (2d Ed.)

The Law of Special Education (2d Ed.)

The Law of Speech and the First Amendment

The Law of Trademarks

The Law of Violence Against Women (2d Ed.)

Lemon Laws

Living Together: Practical Legal Issues

Marriage and Divorce (3d Ed.)

Missing and Exploited Children: How to Protect Your Child

More Everyday Legal Forms

Motor Vehicle and Traffic Law

Nursing Home Negligence

Pet Law

Prescription Drugs

Privacy and the Internet: Your Rights and Expectations Under the Law (2d Ed.)

Probate Law

Protecting Your Business: Disaster Preparation and the Law

Real Estate Law for the Homeowner and Broker (2d Ed.)

Religion and the Law

Retirement Planning

The Right to Die (2d Ed.)

Rights of Single Parents

Small Claims Court

Social Security Law (2d Ed.)

Teenagers and Substance Abuse

Transportation Law: Passenger Rights & Responsibilities

Trouble Next Door: What To Do With Your Neighbor

Veterans' Rights and Benefits

Victim's Rights Law

Welfare: Your Rights and the Law

What If It Happened to You: Violent Crimes and Victims' Rights

What if the Product Doesn't Work: Warranties & Guarantees

Workers' Compensation Law (2d Ed.)

Your Child's Legal Rights: An Overview

Your Rights in a Class Action Suit

Your Rights as a Tenant

Your Rights Under the Family and Medical Leave Act

You've Been Fired: Your Rights and Remedies

INTRODUCTION

This Almanac explores the area of law that governs the obligations and duties owed to passengers by common carriers. A common carrier is generally defined as a business that is licensed to transport passengers and goods. This Almanac focuses on the rights and responsibilities of passengers.

Unlike a private carrier, a common carrier offers its services to the general public. Airlines, railroads, buses and cruise ships operate as common carriers, and are discussed more fully in this Almanac.

This Almanac examines the federal laws that regulate interstate common carriers, and the state laws that regulate intrastate common carriers. In addition, common carrier rules and regulations applicable to passengers are also explored, including rates and fees, property losses and anti-discrimination provisions, including regulations regarding accessibility requirements for passengers with disabilities.

The Appendix provides resource directories, sample forms and other pertinent information and data. The Glossary contains definitions of many of the terms used throughout the Almanac.

CHAPTER 1:
COMMON CARRIERS

WHAT IS A COMMON CARRIER?

A "common carrier" is generally defined as any person or agency publicly engaged in the business of transporting passengers and goods by land, air, or water. Unlike a private carrier, a common carrier offers its services to the general public. The term has also been extended to cover public utility and public service companies.

Common carriers include airlines, railroads, buses, cruise ships, and trucking, as well as telephone, telegraph, and satellite-communication companies. This almanac focuses on those common carriers used to transport passengers, including airlines, railroads, buses, and cruise ships. General information applicable to common carriers can be found below.

GOVERNING AUTHORITY

Common carriers operate pursuant to strict rules and regulations of a federal or state regulatory agency. Regulations generally govern licensing, equipment requirements, procedures, rates, schedules, and routes, and are intended to safeguard the general public. Any changes to a common carrier's rates, schedules, or routes are generally subject to the regulatory agency's approval.

Travel By Land

Interstate Commerce

All common carriers that transport passengers over land in interstate commerce, such as railroads and bus lines, are regulated by the Surface Transportation Board (STB), the successor to the Interstate Commerce Commission. The STB was created by the Interstate Commerce

Commission Termination Act of 1995 to resolve railroad rate and service disputes.

The Interstate Commerce Act—a federal law—governs common carriers that transport passengers or goods across state lines—i.e., interstate transportation. The Interstate Commerce Act regulates the rates and fees charged by a common carrier. Under the Act, a public transportation service must publish its fee schedules to the public, and maintain the published rate. In order to change the published rate, the carrier must first change the published fare schedule and then enforce the new fare rate.

Intrastate Commerce

States laws govern common carriers that operate within state lines—i.e., intrastate transportation. However, such regulations may differ from state to state.

Travel By Air

Airlines are governed by the Federal Aviation Administration (FAA). The FAA is an agency of the U.S. Department of Transportation (DOT), with the authority to regulate and oversee all aspects of civil aviation in the United States.

In addition, the DOT initiated the Essential Air Service program following enactment of the Airline Deregulation Act of 1978. The Airline Deregulation Act gave airlines almost total freedom to determine which markets to serve domestically and what fares to charge for that service.

The purpose of the program is to guarantee that small communities that were served by certificated air carriers before deregulation maintain a minimal level of scheduled air service. Currently, the DOT subsidizes commuter airlines to enable them to serve approximately 140 rural communities across the country that otherwise would not receive any scheduled air service.

Travel By Sea

Cruise ships are governed by the Federal Maritime Commission (FMC). The FMC is an independent regulatory agency responsible for the regulation of ocean-borne transportation.

The FMC oversees the financial responsibility of cruise ship lines and other passenger ship operators, to ensure they have the resources to pay compensation for personal injuries or non-performance.

LIABILITY AND STANDARD OF CARE

Personal Injury

A common carrier is required to use extraordinary care and diligence to provide safe transportation of its passengers. However, a common carrier is not an insurer, thus if the carrier exercises the required degree of care, it will not be liable for all accidents that may occur.

The burden is on the injured passenger to prove that the carrier was negligent in some way, thereby causing the passenger's injuries. However, if the passenger was criminally negligent or violated an express rule of the carrier of which the passenger was aware, it is unlikely that the carrier will be held liable for any injuries sustained by the passenger. A carrier is, however, responsible for any wrongful act committed by an employee that causes injury to a passenger.

Property Damage

In general, a common carrier is liable for any loss or damage to a passenger's property that is being transported. A carrier is not permitted to disclaim such liability by, e.g., placing a liability waiver on the ticket. Nevertheless, a common carrier may be able to limit the amount that a passenger can recover for loss or damage to property.

Statute of Limitations

In most states, a personal injury action involving a common carrier must be filed within a certain period of time from the date of the injury, e.g., 2 years. This law is known as a "statute of limitations." If the injured person does not file his or her lawsuit within this time period, he or she loses the right to recover damages.

In addition, there may also be a requirement that the carrier receive notice of a potential claim as a prerequisite to filing a formal legal action. The required notice of claim must also be filed within a certain period of time, e.g., 6 months. Therefore, it is important to ascertain the applicable statute of limitations, and whether there is a notice of claim prerequisite, when considering suing a common carrier.

RIGHT TO REMOVE PASSENGERS

In general, a common carrier must transport any passenger who has paid his or her fare, subject to space limitations, without discrimination. However, the carrier has the right to remove a passenger who refuses to pay the required fare.

In addition, if the passenger is unruly or otherwise fails to follow the carrier's regulations, he or she may be physically removed from the carrier.

PASSENGERS WITH DISABILITIES

Under the Americans with Disabilities Act of 1990 (ADA), common carriers are required to provide transportation to any individual with a disability. In addition, employees must provide any assistance the individual may need to enter or exit the carrier.

CHAPTER 2:
AIRLINES

IN GENERAL

A number of factors have changed the way people travel by air today. The terrorist attacks of September 11, 2001 resulted in heightened security precautions, and air carriers are experiencing financial constraints, in large part due to the cost of additional security measures, and the rising price of fuel. This chapter sets forth the rights and responsibilities of air travelers and carriers, and the remedies available to address passenger complaints.

OBTAINING THE BEST AIRFARE

Due to price competition among the airlines, it is important to check around to make sure you get the best fare. You can call all of the airlines that service your destination and compare prices. However, it may be easier to obtain this information from a travel agent, who has access to all of the available fares.

In order to find the lowest fare, you must be flexible in your travel plans. For example, the best fares may be offered on flights leaving on certain days of the week or hours of the day. In addition, if there is more than one airport serving your area, the fare may depend on which airport you select. Therefore, you should ask the reservations agent to compare the fares at all of your local airports. You may also save money by taking a flight that has a stopover or connection.

You should also make your plans as early as possible. The lower rates generally sell out quickly. However, an airline may make additional discount fares available at a later date, so it is a good idea to check back periodically prior to the advance purchase deadline.

Before you purchase your ticket, you must inquire about the airline's policy concerning refunds and flight changes. Most discount fares are non-refundable, therefore, if you cannot make your flight, you will lose your money. You may also be charged a fee if you try to change your flight arrangements.

In general, if you make a reservation, but do not purchase the ticket at that time, your fare is not guaranteed. Thus if the fare increases before you purchase the ticket, you will have to pay the higher fee. Some airlines will not increase a fare once the ticket is purchased, however, others may reserve the right to collect any difference prior to departure.

On the other hand, if you find that the fare went down before departure, some airlines will refund the difference. Therefore, it is important that you check the airline's policy in this regard. In addition, if your ticket must be purchased by a specific time or date, this is a deadline. If you don't make the deadline, the airline may cancel your reservations without notice.

MAKING YOUR RESERVATION

Making your flight reservation is fairly easy. You can do so through a travel agent or directly with the airline ticket office. If you plan on traveling during the holidays or other period of high demand, you should make your reservations as early as possible. Many flights are sold out well in advance during busy periods, and the best fares will likely be unavailable if you wait. In addition, if you want to make sure you reach your destination on time, do not purchase a "standby" or "open return" ticket because a seat may not become available during busy travel periods.

To avoid errors, review the flight information with the ticket agent at the time you make your reservation. Ask the ticket agent to confirm the flight numbers, aircraft type, travel dates, destinations, and airports, particularly if there is more than one airport located in your travel area.

When making your reservation, provide your telephone number so you can be contacted ahead of time in case there is a scheduling change. Shortly before your scheduled trip, call the airline to reconfirm your reservation.

Once you receive your ticket, make sure all the information on it is correct. If you find any discrepancies, have the ticket corrected immediately. If your flight involves a change of planes, make sure you have detailed flight information to expedite the transition between planes.

Make sure your name is spelled correctly to avoid confusion regarding your identification. You will be required to show identification with a photograph at the airport, so it is important that the name on your ticket and the name on your identification match. For international flights, make sure the name on your passport and ticket match.

OVERBOOKING

Airlines are permitted to overbook their flights in order to compensate for travelers who do not show up for their flight. When this happens, some passengers may be "bumped"—i.e., excluded—from the flight, either voluntarily or involuntarily.

A table of the number of airline passengers denied boarding, by airline (January–June 2008), can be found in Appendix 1 of this Almanac.

Voluntary Bumping

If overbooking results in an excess of passengers, the Department of Transportation (DOT) requires the airline to ask if there are any passengers who are willing to voluntarily give up their seat in exchange for compensation and a later flight before they can involuntarily bump a passenger. If you decide to give up your seat, you should first find out when the next flight with a confirmed seat will be available. If there will be a long delay, you should also find out whether the airline will provide food and lodging in addition to any compensation offered.

The DOT does not set the amount of compensation the airline must give you. The airline is free to negotiate the compensation, which may be in the form of money, a free ticket, or some other type of compensation. If you are offered a free ticket, ask whether there are any restrictions or limitations associated with the ticket, such as an expiration date or blackout periods when you would not be permitted to travel.

Involuntary Bumping

If there are no passengers willing to voluntarily give up their seat, and passengers must be left behind involuntarily, the DOT requires the airline to give the affected passengers a written statement that sets forth their rights and explains how the airline decides who gets bumped from the flight.

For example, some airlines bump passengers who hold the lowest fares first. For passengers in the same fare class, the last passengers to check in are usually the first to be bumped, even if they have met the check-in deadline. Therefore, it is advisable to get to the airport early.

Often, the airline will compensate you for the price of the ticket and the length of the delay. This payment is known as "denied boarding compensation," which is given to compensate you for your inconvenience.

In addition to the compensation received, you are entitled to keep your original ticket and use it on another flight. If you make your own substitute flight arrangements, you can request an "involuntary refund" for your original ticket.

Substitute Flights

If the airline is able to arrange a substitute flight, the airline may not have to compensate you, depending on the extent of the delay, as follows:

1. If the substitute flight will arrive at the destination within one hour after the original arrival time, the airline is not required to compensate you.

2. If the substitute flight will arrive at the destination between one and two hours after the original arrival time, or between one and four hours on international flights, the airline must pay you an amount equal to your one-way fare, with a maximum of $400.

3. If the substitute flight will arrive at the destination more than two hours after the original arrival time, or after four hours for international flights, the airline must pay you an amount double your fare, with a maximum of $800.

4. If the airline does not make any substitute travel arrangements, the airline must pay you an amount double your fare, with a maximum of $800.

Eligibility

There are certain conditions that apply in order for you to be eligible to receive compensation:

1. You must have a confirmed reservation.

2. You must buy your ticket by the purchase deadline.

3. You must meet the airline's check-in deadline, which may require you to be at the ticket counter or boarding area a certain number of hours prior to the scheduled departure time.

If you miss the ticketing or check-in deadline, you may lose both your reservation and your right to compensation if the flight is oversold.

Exceptions

There are also certain exceptions that apply to the compensation requirement:

1. No compensation is due if the airline arranges substitute transportation, which is scheduled to arrive at your destination within one hour of your originally scheduled arrival time.

2. If the airline must substitute a smaller plane for the one it originally planned to use, the carrier is not required to compensate you.

3. On flights using aircraft with 30 through 60 passenger seats, compensation is not required if you were bumped due to safety-related aircraft weight or balance constraints.

4. Compensation rules do not apply to charter flights.

5. Compensation rules do not apply to scheduled flights on planes that hold fewer than 30 passengers.

6. Compensation rules do not apply to international flights inbound to the United States.

7. Compensation rules do not apply to flights between two foreign cities.

TICKETING

Refunds

Generally, you may purchase your ticket using cash, a check or a credit card. If you purchased a refundable ticket, and paid in cash, you can typically get an immediate refund from the travel agency or airline. If you paid by check, your refund will be sent by mail after your check has cleared the bank.

If you purchase your ticket with a credit card, your account is billed even if you do not use your tickets. In order to have the fare credited to your account, you will typically have to return the original unused ticket to the airline. An advantage to paying by credit card is the protection you have under federal law. The airline must send a credit to the credit card company within seven business days after receiving a refund application. If you do not see the credit on your statement, write to the credit card company within 60 days from the date the company mailed you the statement on which the airline fare was charged. The credit card company should credit your account whether or not the airline has sent the credit.

Further, if you change your flight after having purchased your ticket, ask the ticket agent to apply the amount you already paid toward the new ticket, and charge or credit any difference in the prices. This is preferable to having your account double-billed, and saves you the trouble of having to seek a refund for the first ticket.

Lost or Stolen Tickets

Unfortunately, if your ticket is lost or stolen, obtaining a replacement ticket or a refund may be more difficult than expected. To avoid a delay in obtaining a replacement or refund, you should write down the ticket number and keep it separate from your ticket. You should report the loss or theft to the issuing airline immediately. If you have the ticket number, the airline may be able to issue a replacement ticket immediately, or process an expedited refund.

In some cases, you may have to purchase a replacement ticket, particularly if you need the ticket to continue your travel. To make matters worse, the discounted fare you originally purchased may no longer be available, so the replacement ticket will cost more. However, if you do not make any changes to your original flight, the airline should give you a refund for the higher priced ticket. Processing your refund may take anywhere from two to six months, particularly if someone has tried to use your ticket in the meantime.

Contract Terms

Each airline has specific rules that make up your contract. These rules may differ among airlines, and include provisions such as check-in deadlines, refund procedures, responsibility for delayed flights, etc.

Domestic Travel

For domestic travel, an airline may provide all of the contract terms on or with your ticket at the time of purchase. Some airlines do not provide all of the airline's rules with the ticket but "incorporate terms by reference." This means that the terms are contained in a separate document, which you may inspect on request.

If the airline chooses this method, it must provide conspicuous written notice with each ticket that: (1) it incorporates terms by reference; and (2) the "incorporated by reference" terms may include liability limitations, claim-filing deadlines, check-in deadlines, and certain other key terms. In addition, the airline must:

1. ensure that passengers can receive an explanation of key terms identified on the ticket from any location where the carrier's tickets are sold, including travel agencies;

2. make the full text of its contract available for inspection at each of its own airport and city ticket offices;

3. mail a free copy of the full text of its contract upon request.

Further, there are additional notice requirements for contract terms that affect your airfare. Thus airlines must provide a conspicuous written notice on or with the ticket concerning any "incorporated" contract terms that:

1. restrict refunds;

2. impose monetary penalties; or

3. permit the airline to raise the price after you've bought the ticket.

If an airline incorporates contract terms by reference and fails to provide the required notice about a particular rule, the passenger will not be bound by that rule.

International Travel

For international travel, the detailed requirements for disclosing domestic contract terms do not apply. Airlines file "tariff rules" with the government for this transportation, and passengers are generally bound by these rules whether or not they receive actual notice about them. Every international airline must keep a copy of its tariff rules at its airport and city ticket offices.

You have the right to examine the airline's tariff rules. In addition, the airline agents must answer your questions about information in the tariff, and they must help you locate specific tariff rules, if necessary. If the airline keeps its tariff rules in a computer rather than on paper, there are additional disclosure requirements, which are similar to those for domestic contract terms.

The most important point to remember, whether your travel is domestic or international, is that you should not be afraid to ask questions about a carrier's rules. You have a right to know the terms of your contract.

DELAYS AND CANCELLATIONS

Flight delays and cancellations can occur for a number of reasons. According to the Air Travel Consumer Report, the overall causes of delay, as reported by the airline carriers in June 2008, included:

1. National aviation system delay—10.16%

2. Late arriving aircraft delay—8.86%

3. Air carrier delay—6.78%

4. Cancellations—1.8%

5. Extreme weather delay—1.14%

6. Diverted flight—0.37%

7. Security delay—0.05%

The on-time performance rate for the airlines was 70.84%.

Flight delays and cancellations can spoil a trip. And unless the airline is at fault—e.g., for overbooking the flight—it may not provide any amenities to stranded passengers. Airlines are not required to compensate passengers when flights are delayed or cancelled, and there are no federal laws that require an airline to provide food or lodging to stranded passengers. Therefore, if you absolutely need to be at your destination on time, you should plan to leave early enough to account for any delays.

Many airlines maintain an on-time performance record for their flights. If you are concerned about possible delays, when you make your reservation, you should ask the ticket agent for the on-time performance code of the flights you are considering. This is a one-digit code that indicates how often a particular flight has arrived on time—within 15 minutes—during the most recently reported month. If the flights you are considering are comparable in other respects, you may want to travel on the flight that has the best on-time performance record.

A table of the number of flight delays, by airline (June 2008), can be found in Appendix 2 of this Almanac.

It is more likely that a later flight will be subject to delays or cancellations than an early flight. This is because any problems throughout the day may start to pile up and affect subsequent flights. In addition, if you reserve the last flight of the day, and it is cancelled, you will likely have to wait overnight for the next available flight.

When reserving your flight, you should consider whether a connecting flight—i.e., a flight that requires a change of planes—will be more likely to cause scheduling problems than a direct flight. For example, you should take into account the potential for bad weather in the connecting city that could lead to a delay or cancellation of the connecting flight.

You should also determine the amount of time between the arrival time of your first flight and the departure time of your connecting flight. If there is any delay in your first flight, you may miss your connecting flight as a result. If you must reach your destination on time, you may want to book a direct flight to avoid the potential for delay.

BAGGAGE HANDLING

Carry-On Luggage

Your carry-on bag must meet the size limitations for all airlines with which you plan to travel, as policies may vary. The maximum size carry-on bag for most airlines is 45 linear inches, including (the total height, width and depth of the bag). Anything larger must generally be checked in the cargo department.

Liquids, Gels and Aerosols

Passengers are permitted to carry liquids, gels and aerosols in their carry-on bag; however, the following rules apply to all such items carried through security checkpoints:

1. All liquids, gels and aerosols must be in three-ounce or smaller containers.

2. All liquids, gels and aerosols must be placed in a single, quart-size, zip-top, clear plastic bag.

3. Each passenger must remove their quart-sized plastic, zip-top bag from their carry-on bag and place it in a bin or on the conveyor belt for X-ray screening.

There are exceptions to the "3 ounce" rule for the health and welfare of certain passengers provided the items are presented to the security officer at the checkpoint. These items must be in a reasonable quantity and may include:

1. baby formula, breast milk and juice for infants and toddlers;

2. all prescription and over-the-counter medications in liquid, gel or aerosol form, including petroleum jelly, eye drops and saline solution for medical purposes only;

3. liquids, including water, juice or liquid nutrition, or gels for passengers with a disability or medical condition;

4. life-support and life-sustaining liquids such as bone marrow, blood products and transplant organs;

5. items used to augment the body for medical or cosmetic reasons such as mastectomy products, prosthetic breasts, bras or shells containing gels, saline solution or other liquids; and

6. frozen gels and liquids are permitted if required to cool for medical and infant/child exemptions, but for no other purpose.

Illegal and Hazardous Items

There are certain illegal and hazardous items that you cannot carry on board the plane or in your checked luggage. This includes explosive and flammable materials, and disabling chemicals. A violation of the hazardous materials restrictions can result in a civil penalty of up to $25,000 for each violation, or a criminal penalty of up to $500,000 and/or up to 5 years in jail.

Checked Luggage

The luggage you check is also subject to size, weight, and excess baggage limitations. If you exceed the airline's limit, you may be charged extra.

For safety reasons, there are certain items that you should not pack in your check-in luggage, including:

1. valuables, such as cash or jewelry;

2. critical items, such as medicine, passport, keys, important papers;

3. irreplaceable items, such as heirlooms or manuscripts;

4. fragile items, such as glass containers, eyeglasses, breakable items; and

5. perishable items.

These types of items should be in your carry-on bag or on your person. However, if you have to pack fragile items in your checked luggage, make sure you place the items in secure, durable packaging because bags often get tossed around in transit. In addition, label all of your checked luggage with your contact information.

If you are late checking in, your luggage may not get on the same flight with you, in which case the airline may decline liability if it is lost or delayed. If possible, select a nonstop flight, or a direct flight that does not require a change of planes. The potential for loss or delay increases when your travel plans require a change in planes.

When you check your baggage, the airline will place destination tags on your luggage and give you a claim check for each bag. The tags contain a three-letter airport code and flight number identifying your destination. Make sure this information is accurate before your baggage is taken away.

Keep the claim checks in a safe place until you reclaim your baggage at your destination and check the contents to make sure your property is intact. If any of your property is missing or damaged, and you want to make a formal claim, you will need the claim check. In addition, some airports will not let you leave the baggage claim area with your luggage without first showing your claim checks. Make sure you remove the destination tags from your bags before you get on another flight to avoid any confusion and misdirected luggage.

Lost or Damaged Luggage

Considering the volume of luggage that airlines handle daily, they actually have a pretty good record when it comes to baggage handling.

A table of the number of mishandled baggage reports, by airline (January–June 2008), can be found in Appendix 3 of this Almanac.

Nevertheless, on occasion, luggage will get lost, delayed, damaged, or stolen. If your luggage, or the contents, is damaged, the airline will generally compensate you for your loss. However, if you carelessly packed a fragile item, the airline will likely deny your claim. In addition, the airline may disclaim liability for damaged property inside your luggage when there is no visible exterior damage to the luggage.

If your luggage does not reach your destination with you, report the missing luggage immediately before you leave the airport. Fill out the appropriate form and request a copy, along with a telephone number you can call to follow up on your lost luggage claim. In most cases, your luggage will be found and returned to you within a matter of hours. The airline may compensate you for the inconvenience caused by the delay. Find out what items you may be reimbursed for, such as toiletries and other necessities, and keep copies of your receipts.

If your luggage cannot be found, you will have to file a more detailed claim with the airline, with details about your lost property. The airline will use this information to place a value on your loss, taking into account any depreciation. If you are claiming the loss of any valuables, the airline will request documentation for the value of the items. Once you have negotiated a mutually agreeable settlement of your claim, the airline will reimburse you for the loss up to its liability limitation.

Domestic Flights

On domestic flights, an airline can limit its liability for lost or damaged luggage to a maximum of $3,000. If the contents of your luggage are particularly valuable, you may want to purchase "excess valuation" coverage when you check in. However, the airline has the right to refuse this coverage if the items are exceptionally fragile or costly.

If the depreciated value of your property is worth less than the liability limit, you will be offered the lesser amount. If the airline's settlement doesn't fully reimburse you for your loss, you may be able to recover an additional amount under your homeowner policy.

International Flights

On international roundtrip flights that originate in the United States, the airline's liability for lost or damaged luggage is governed by the Montreal Convention. This treaty also governs liability on international roundtrips that originate in another country that has ratified the Montreal Convention, and one-way trips between the United States and the ratifying country. The international limit also applies to domestic segments of an international journey.

The airline's liability on such flights is limited to 1,000 "Special Drawing Rights" (SDR) per passenger. The value of one SDR in terms of United States dollars is determined daily by the International Monetary Fund, based on the exchange rates of the major currencies used in international trade and finance (the "basket"). At present, the currencies in the basket are the euro, the pound sterling, the Japanese yen, and the U.S. dollar.

SMOKING BAN

Smoking is prohibited on all domestic flights, except for flights over six hours to or from Alaska or Hawaii. This ban applies to domestic segments of international flights, on both U.S. and foreign airlines. The smoking ban does not apply to nonstop international flights, even during the time that they are in U.S. airspace. Cigar and pipe smoking is banned on all U.S. carrier flights. The following rules apply to U.S. airlines on flights where smoking is permitted, e.g., on international flights:

1. The airline must provide a seat in a non-smoking section to every passenger who asks for one, as long as the passenger complies with the carrier's seat assignment deadline and procedures.

2. If necessary, the airline must expand the non-smoking section to accommodate the passengers described above.

3. The airline does not have to provide a non-smoking seat of the passenger's choice.

4. The airline is not required to provide advance seat assignments before the flight date in the non-smoking section, as long as they get the passenger into the non-smoking section on the day of the flight.

5. The flight crew must keep passengers from smoking in the non-smoking sections. However, smoke that drifts from the smoking section into the non-smoking section does not constitute a violation.

6. No smoking is allowed while an aircraft is on the ground or when the ventilation system is not fully functioning.

7. Carriers are not required to have a smoking section. An airline is free to ban smoking on a particular flight, or on all of its flights.

STAYING SAFE DURING TURBULENCE

Turbulence during a flight occurs when there is unexpected air movement caused by atmospheric pressure, jet streams, thunderstorms, etc. Turbulence can be dangerous, particularly if you are not wearing your seatbelt. Approximately two-thirds of turbulence-related accidents occur at or above 30,000 feet.

The FAA has addressed these concerns by issuing regulations that require passengers to remain seated with their seatbelts fastened during the following:

1. when the airplane leaves the gate and as it climbs after take-off;

2. during landing and taxi; and

3. whenever the seatbelt sign is illuminated during the flight.

It is important to follow these safety regulations because in-flight turbulence is the leading cause of injuries to airline passengers and flight attendants. Each year, approximately 58 passengers in the United States are injured by turbulence while not wearing seatbelts.

Child Safety During Turbulence

The safest place for a small child during turbulence is in an approved child restraint system (CRS). A CRS is a hard-backed child safety seat that is approved by the government for use in aircraft and motor vehicles.

In addition, the Federal Aviation Administration (FAA) has approved a harness-type restraint appropriate for children weighing between 22 and 44 pounds. This type of device provides an alternative to using a hard-backed seat and is approved only for use on an aircraft.

TRAVELING WITH PETS

The FAA allows each airline to decide if they will allow pets to travel in the passenger cabin. Thus if you plan on traveling with your pet, you should first ask the airline whether they permit pets to travel in the passenger cabin. If so, the pet container is considered carry-on luggage, and must meet the following requirements:

1. The pet container must be small enough to fit underneath the seat without blocking any person's path to the main aisle of the airplane.

2. The pet container must be stowed properly before the last passenger entry door to the airplane is closed in order for the airplane to leave the gate.

3. The pet container must remain properly stowed the entire time the airplane is moving on the airport surface, and for take off and landing.

4. Passengers must follow the flight attendant's instructions regarding the proper stowage of the pet container.

In addition, the airline may limit the types and number of pets that can be brought into the cabin; require that the pet be harmless, inoffensive, and odorless; and require that the pet remain in the pet container for the entire flight. In addition, you may be required to produce a recently issued health certificate for your pet.

Passengers with Pet Allergies

Passengers who are allergic to pets may want to reduce the chance that they will have an allergic reaction in-flight by flying on an airline that does not allow pets in the passenger cabin. However, as discussed in Chapter 2, "Airlines," of this Almanac, airlines are required to allow disabled passengers to bring their service animals in the passenger cabin. Service animals are not considered pets.

In addition, passengers with severe allergies may still be exposed to pet dander because most allergens are carried into the cabin on the clothing of other passengers. Therefore, before flying, ask your medical provider whether you should carry your medication with you. If you have an allergic reaction during the flight, follow your medical provider's treatment instructions and ask the flight attendant for assistance.

UNACCOMPANIED MINORS

Children are permitted to fly alone, however, airlines have established specific procedures to protect unaccompanied minors. Most U.S. airlines permit children who have reached their fifth birthday to travel alone. Children under the age of 5 must travel with someone at least 12 years of age (or 18 on some airlines). Children age 5 through 11 (or 14 on some airlines) must generally travel pursuant to special "unaccompanied minor" procedures, for a fee. Many airlines will only allow children age 5 through 7 to fly on nonstop flights.

Some airlines do not have unaccompanied minor procedures for children age 12 to 17 (or 15 to 17 on some airlines), and considers such children to be "young adult" passengers. However, the airline will apply those procedures at the request of the parent or guardian, for a fee. If unaccompanied minor arrangements are not made, the child will generally be responsible for making his or her own alternative plans in the event of a canceled, diverted, or delayed flight, and the parent or guardian will not necessarily be notified should this occur.

On international flights, children age 12 to 17 (or 15 to 17 on some airlines) can travel alone on any flight, but most airlines will require they travel pursuant to unaccompanied minor procedures. Children must have the same passport, visa, or other international entry documentation as an adult. It is advisable to check with the U.S. embassy or consulate in the designated country for any additional requirements.

It is preferable to book a nonstop flight for a child who is traveling alone. Some airlines don't allow unaccompanied minors on connecting flights. Standby travel is generally not permitted. Check the child's ticket for accuracy. Request a gate pass so that you can accompany the child to the departure gate. Each adult going to the gate must have a government-issued photo ID.

In addition to airfare, most airlines charge a fee for unaccompanied minor services, ranging from $50 to $100 each way. The fee may be higher for international flights. An airline employee will escort the child off the airplane at the destination. The person designated to meet the child at the destination should bring a government-issued photo ID. The airline will only release the child to the person designated on the Unaccompanied Minor form.

PERSONAL INJURY COMPLAINTS

In general, the airline is liable for injuries sustained by its passengers. In fact, because of the special relationship that exists between the airline and it passengers, the airline is held to a higher standard of safeguarding its passengers. In fact, the airline is required to take the highest degree of care in protecting passengers from harm.

Further, the airline also has a duty to warn its passengers of any known dangers that exist. If the passenger is made aware, yet ignores the warning, the carrier may not be found liable, or may only be found partially liable for the passenger's injuries.

For example, if an airline passenger is told that he or she must remain seated and belted during turbulence for safety reasons, and the passenger ignores the warning, gets out of his or her seat, walks down the aisle, and falls to the floor, the airline may escape liability for any injuries the passenger sustained as a result of the fall.

This duty of care begins when the passenger boards the aircraft and does not end until the passenger departs. During this time, airlines must do everything reasonably possible to prevent injury to its passengers and make sure they arrive at their destination safely.

Although an airline may require its passengers to sign a waiver limiting its liability for such things as lost baggage, it is against public policy to require its passengers to waive liability for negligently causing injury to its passenger. Such a waiver will not be upheld in court.

Domestic Travel

If you suffer an injury while on the airplane, e.g., you slip and fall, or you are struck by falling baggage from the overhead bin—you may be able to file a claim against the airline for negligence. If you have been injured on an airplane, you should consult a personal injury attorney experienced in aviation accidents to discuss whether you have a claim against the airline.

You must file your personal injury lawsuit within the time period set forth in the applicable statute of limitations. If you do not file the lawsuit within the applicable time period, you will lose the right to sue the airline for your injuries. Therefore, it is imperative that you determine which statute of limitations applies to your particular situation.

International Travel

As it relates to international travel, the United States adheres to the "Warsaw Convention" which provides that an air carrier's liability for a negligent act causing personal injury to one of its passengers, is limited to 125,000 francs—approximately $8,300—for each passenger. If the air carrier is guilty of "willful misconduct" or if a special contract has been entered into, the limitation does not apply.

The Warsaw Convention requires the injured party to bring a lawsuit within two years of the accident or the action will be dismissed. Also, the air carrier will not be liable if the carrier can prove that due care was used. This Act applies to injuries sustained on the plane or while embarking or disembarking from an international flight.

The Montreal Agreement increases the liability amounts under the Warsaw Convention. Pursuant to the Montreal Agreement, many carriers agreed to increase their liability limits up to $75,000, including legal fees, while also waiving their right to a defense that due care was used by the carrier. These increased liability limits apply to flights starting, ending or having a stopping place within the United States.

FLIGHT COMPLAINTS

If you have a complaint concerning your flight, you should first try to deal directly with the customer service department of the airline located at the airport. Often the customer service representatives can resolve your problem. However, if you cannot resolve the problem at the airport, and want to file a complaint, you should contact the airline's consumer office at the corporate headquarters.

You should file your complaint, in writing, and include the following information, as applicable:

1. your contact information;

2. details concerning the event you are complaining about, including dates, cities, flight numbers, flight times, etc.;

3. copies of your ticket, receipts or other documentation supporting your claim;

4. names of employees who you believe were responsible for the problem;

5. details of any losses you suffered as a result of the problem;

6. the compensation you believe you are entitled to as a result of the problem.

Your letter will help the airline determine what caused your problem, and how best to handle your complaint.

A directory of airline customer relations departments can be found in Appendix 4 of this Almanac.

Common complaint categories include the following:

1. Flight Problems—Cancellations, delays, or any other deviations from schedule, whether planned or unplanned.

2. Oversales—All bumping problems, whether or not the airline complied with DOT oversales regulations.

3. Reservations, Ticketing, and Boarding—Airline or travel agent mistakes made in reservations and ticketing; problems in making reservations and obtaining tickets due to busy telephone lines or waiting in line, or delays in mailing tickets; problems boarding the aircraft, not including oversales.

4. Fares—Incorrect or incomplete information about fares, discount fare conditions and availability, overcharges, fare increases and level of fares in general.

5. Refunds—Problems in obtaining refunds for unused or lost tickets, fare adjustments, or bankruptcies.

6. Baggage—Claims for lost, damaged or delayed baggage, charges for excess baggage, carry-on problems, and difficulties with airline claims procedures.

7. Customer Service—Rude or unhelpful employees, inadequate meals or cabin service, treatment of delayed passengers.

8. Disability—Civil rights complaints by air travelers with disabilities.

9. Advertising—Advertising that is unfair, misleading or offensive to consumers.

10. Discrimination—Civil rights complaints by air travelers (other than disability); for example, complaints based on race, national origin, religion, etc.

11. Animals—Loss, injury or death of an animal during air transport provided by an air carrier.

12. Other—Frequent flyer, smoking, tours credit, cargo problems, security, airport facilities, claims for bodily injury, and others not classified above.

A table of the number of airline complaints filed, by category (January–June 2008), can be found in Appendix 5 of this Almanac.

If you choose to file a complaint about airline service with the Department of Transportation, you may do so in writing or online with the Aviation Consumer Protection Division, as follows:

Aviation Consumer Protection Division
U.S. Department of Transportation
1200 New Jersey Ave, S.E.
Washington, D.C. 20590
Tel: 202-366-2220
Website: http://airconsumer.ost.dot.gov/escomplaint/es.cfm/

The U.S. Department of Transportation Air Travel Complaint Form can be found in Appendix 6 of this Almanac.

If your complaint is concerns a safety or security hazard, you can write or call the Federal Aviation Administration, as follows:

Assistant Administrator for System Safety
Federal Aviation Administration
800 Independence Avenue, S.W.
Washington, D.C. 20591
Tel: 800-FAA-SURE

A table of the number of consumer complaints filed, by airline (January–June 2008), can be found in Appendix 7 of this Almanac.

CHECKPOINT SCREENING COMPLAINTS

Since the terrorist attacks against the United States on September 11, 2001, the airlines have had to take extra precautions in screening passengers to protect the safety of the traveling public. Screening is required to be conducted in a manner free from unlawful discrimination, harassment or retaliation.

Passengers who believe they have been treated differently or unfairly by security screening officers because of their race, national origin, age, religion, gender, disability or sexual orientation can file a civil rights or civil liberties complaint, as set forth below.

During travel, while still at the checkpoint, ask to speak with a supervisor or the Customer Service Manager for the airport. After traveling, you may file a complaint with the Transportation Security Administration (TSA) Office of Civil Rights and Liberties at the following address:

> Transportation Security Administration
> Office of Civil Rights and Liberties
> External Compliance Division
> 601 S. 12th Street
> Arlington, Virginia 22202
> E-mail: TSA.OCR-ExternalCompliance@dhs.gov/

Your complaint should include the date and approximate time of the incident; the name of the airline carrier; the name of the airport; and a description of what happened. Explain why you feel you were discriminated against.

A specialist will be handled to investigate your complaint. The Office of Civil Rights and Liberties will review the facts and make findings as to whether or not the incident complained of constituted unlawful discrimination, harassment or retaliation, and may recommend measures to be put in place to resolve the concern.

You may also contact the Department of Homeland Security (DHS) Office for Civil Rights and Civil Liberties to file a complaint. DHS procedures for filing and handling complaints are located on the DHS website at: http://www.dhs.gov/.

CHAPTER 3:
RIGHTS OF AIR TRAVELERS WITH DISABILITIES

THE AIR CARRIER ACCESS ACT

More than 17 million persons with disabilities in the United States travel by air each year. In 1986, recognizing the difficulties persons with disabilities faced when traveling by air, Congress passed the Air Carrier Access Act (14 CFR Part 382). The Air Carrier Access Act required the Department of Transportation (DOT) to develop new regulations to ensure that persons with disabilities would be treated without discrimination.

The DOT rules were published in March 1990 and have been amended several times since then. The rules are designed to protect the rights of airline passengers with disabilities. The rules have done away with many of the restrictions that used to discriminate against disabilities, as follows:

1. An air carrier may not refuse transportation to a passenger solely on the basis of a disability.

2. Air carriers may not limit the number of individuals with disabilities on a particular flight.

3. All trip information that is made available to other passengers also must be made available to passengers with disabilities.

4. Air carriers must provide passage to an individual who has a disability that may affect his or her appearance or involuntary behavior, even if this disability may offend, annoy, or be an inconvenience to crewmembers or other passengers.

Exceptions

There are certain exceptions to the DOT rules, as follows:

1. The air carrier may refuse transportation if the individual with a disability would endanger the health or safety of other passengers, or transporting the person would be a violation of Federal Aviation Administration (FAA) safety rules.

2. The carrier may refuse transportation if there are no lifts, boarding chairs or similar devices available that can be adapted to board the passenger. Airline personnel are not required to physically carry a mobility-impaired person on or off the aircraft. Lifts, boarding chairs or similar devices are currently required for nearly all flights on aircraft with 19 or more seats at airports with 10,000 or more annual enplanements.

3. There are special rules about persons with certain disabilities or communicable diseases, as discussed below.

4. The air carrier may refuse transportation if it is unable to seat the passenger without violating the FAA exit row seating rules, as discussed below.

RIGHT TO ADVANCE INFORMATION

Upon request, air travelers with disabilities must be provided advance information concerning facilities and services available to them and, if possible, information about the specific aircraft. Such information includes:

1. any limitations concerning the ability of the aircraft to accommodate an individual with a disability;

2. the location of seats with movable aisle armrests, if any, and the location of seats which the carrier does not make available to an individual with a disability, such as exit rows;

3. any limitations on the availability of storage facilities in the cabin or in the cargo bay for mobility aids, or other equipment commonly used by an individual with a disability; and

4. whether the aircraft has an accessible lavatory.

Typically, advance information about an aircraft is provided over the telephone. Under the rules, any carrier that takes reservations or information over the telephone must provide comparable services for hearing-impaired individuals. This can be accomplished by using telecommunication devices for the deaf (TDDs) or text telephones (TTs).

The air carrier may not require air travelers with disabilities to provide advance notice of their disabilities, except under the following conditions:

1. Air carriers may require up to 48 hours advance notice and one hour advance check-in from a person with a disability who wishes to receive any of the following services:

(a) transportation for an electric wheelchair on an aircraft with fewer than 60 seats;

(b) provision by the carrier of hazardous materials packaging for the battery of a wheelchair or other assistive device;

(c) accommodations for 10 or more passengers with disabilities who travel as a group; and

(d) provision of an on-board wheelchair on an aircraft that does not have an accessible lavatory for persons who can use an inaccessible lavatory but need an on-board wheelchair to do so.

2. An airline that uses block seating for passengers with disabilities may require 24 hours advance notice for these accommodations.

3. Although not required, a carrier who chooses to provide the following optional services or equipments may require 48 hours advance notice and a one hour advance check-in:

(a) medical oxygen;

(b) an incubator;

(c) hook-up for a respirator to the aircraft's electrical supply; and

(d) accommodations for a passenger who must travel on a stretcher.

In addition, air carriers may impose reasonable, non-discriminatory charges for these optional services.

4. Where a service is required by the rules, the carrier must ensure that it is provided if appropriate notice has been given and the service requested is available on that particular flight. If a passenger does not meet advance notice or check-in requirements, carriers must make a reasonable effort to accommodate the requested service, providing this does not delay the flight.

5. If a passenger with a disability provides the required notice but is required to fly on another carrier, e.g., if the original flight is cancelled, the original carrier must, to the maximum extent feasible,

provide assistance to the second carrier in furnishing the accommodation requested by the individual.

ATTENDANT REQUIREMENT

An air carrier may require the following individuals to be accompanied by an attendant:

1. a person traveling on a stretcher or in an incubator;

2. a person who, because of a mental disability, is unable to comprehend or respond appropriately to safety instructions from carrier personnel;

3. a person with a mobility impairment so severe that the individual is unable to assist in his or her own evacuation from the aircraft;

4. a person who has both severe hearing and severe vision impairments which prevent him or her from receiving and acting on necessary instructions from carrier personnel when evacuating the aircraft during an emergency.

If the carrier and the passenger disagree as to whether an attendant is required, the carrier can still require an attendant. This could be accomplished as follows:

1. the airline could designate an off-duty employee who happened to be traveling on the same flight to act as the attendant;

2. the carrier or the passenger with a disability could seek a volunteer from among other passengers on the flight to act as the attendant; or

3. the carrier could provide a free ticket to an attendant of the passenger's choice for that flight segment.

The attendant would not be required to provide any personal services to the passenger except to assist the passenger in case of an emergency evacuation. If the carrier arranges for an attendant, the carrier cannot charge the passenger for this service. In any event, the carrier is not required to find or furnish an attendant.

If a person with a disability holding a confirmed reservation is denied travel on the flight because there is no seat available for an attendant, the passenger is eligible for denied boarding compensation, as discussed in Chapter 1, "Common Carriers," of this Almanac.

AIRPORT ACCESSIBILITY GUIDELINES

Under the Air Carrier Access rules and the Americans with Disabilities Act of 1990 (ADA), airport facilities must comply with federal ADA

Accessibility Guidelines (ADAAG). In general, the following services should be available in all air carrier terminals:

1. accessible parking near the terminal;

2. signs indicating accessible parking and the easiest access from those spaces to the terminal;

3. accessible medical aid facilities and travelers aid stations;

4. accessible restrooms;

5. accessible drinking fountains;

6. accessible ticketing systems at primary fare collection areas;

7. amplified telephones and text telephones for use by persons with hearing and speech impairments;

8. accessible baggage check-in and retrieval areas;

9. jet bridges and mobile lounges which are accessible at airports that have such facilities;

10. level entry boarding ramps, lifts or other means of assisting an individual with a disability on and off an aircraft;

11. information systems using visual words, letters or symbols with lighting and color coding, and systems for providing information orally; and

12. signs indicating the location of specific facilities and services.

RIGHT TO FLIGHT INFORMATION

Air carriers must ensure that, upon request, individuals with disabilities are supplied with the same flight information provided to other passengers regarding the following:

1. ticketing;

2. scheduled departure times and gates;

3. change of gate assignments;

4. status of flight delays;

5. schedule changes;

6. flight check-in;

7. checking and claiming of luggage.

In addition, a copy of the Air Carrier Access rules must be made available by carriers for inspection upon request at each airport.

SECURITY SCREENING

A passenger with a disability is required to undergo the same security screening as any other passenger. If the passenger is able to pass through the security system without activating it, he or she shall not be subject to special screening procedures.

If the passenger is not able to pass through the system without activating it, he or she will be subject to further screening in the same manner as any other passenger activating the system. Security screening personnel at some airports may employ a hand-held device that will allow them to complete the screening without having to physically search the individual.

If this method is still unable to clear the individual and a physical search becomes necessary, then at the passenger's request, the search must be done in private. If the passenger requests a private screening in a timely manner, the carrier must provide it in time for the passenger to board the aircraft.

In addition, security personnel are permitted to examine an assistive device that they believe is capable of concealing a weapon or other prohibited item.

MEDICAL CERTIFICATE REQUIREMENT

A medical certificate may be required for persons with certain conditions or communicable diseases. A medical certificate is a written statement from the passenger's physician saying that the passenger is capable of completing the flight safely without requiring extraordinary medical care.

Conditions Requiring a Medical Certificate

A disability alone is not sufficient grounds for a carrier to request a medical certificate. Air carriers shall not require passengers to present a medical certificate unless the person:

(a) is on a stretcher or in an incubator;

(b) needs medical oxygen during flight;

(c) has a medical condition which causes the carrier to have reasonable doubt that the individual can complete the flight safely, without requiring extraordinary medical assistance during the flight; or

(d) has a communicable disease or infection that has been determined by federal public health authorities to be generally transmittable during flight.

Communicable Disease

As part of their responsibility to their passengers, air carriers try to prevent the spread of infection or a communicable disease on board an aircraft. Thus if a medical certificate is necessitated by a communicable disease, the air carrier may:

1. refuse to provide transportation to the person;

2. require the person to provide a medical certificate stating that the disease at its current stage would not be transmittable during the normal course of flight, or describing measures which would prevent transmission during flight; or

3. impose on the person a condition or requirement not imposed on other passengers, such as requiring the passenger to wear a mask.

In any event, if the passenger has a contagious disease, but presents a medical certificate describing conditions or precautions that would prevent the transmission of the disease during the flight, the carrier must allow the passenger to travel unless the carrier is unable to comply with the conditions or precautions set forth in the certificate.

RIGHT TO A SAFETY BRIEFING

Air carrier personnel provide a safety briefing to all passengers before takeoff. Passengers with disabilities are entitled to the same briefing. If the passenger's disability prevents him or her from understanding the information, e.g., because of a vision or hearing disability, the carrier may provide the passenger with an individual safety briefing.

The briefing must be given in a discrete manner, e.g., during pre-boarding of passengers with disabilities. If the carrier presents the safety briefing on a video screen, there must be captions for the hearing-impaired or an insert for a sign language interpreter.

Nevertheless, a carrier may not take any adverse action against the passenger because the passenger was unable to understand the safety briefing.

RIGHT TO BRING MOBILITY AIDS AND ASSISTIVE DEVICES ON BOARD

Stowage

Disabled passengers have the right to bring mobility aids and assistive devices on board the aircraft, with certain limitations. In addition, assistive devices do not count toward a limit on carry-on items. Carriers must permit one folding wheelchair to be stowed in an approved storage area,

RIGHTS OF AIR TRAVELERS WITH DISABILITIES

if the aircraft has such areas and stowage can be accomplished in accordance with FAA safety regulations.

If the passenger using the wheelchair pre-boards, stowage of the wheelchair takes priority over the carry-on items brought on by other passengers getting on the airplane at the same airport, including first class passengers, but does not take priority over items of passengers who boarded at previous stops.

When stowed in the cargo compartment, wheelchairs and other assistive devices take priority over cargo and baggage, and must be among the first items unloaded. Such mobility aids must be returned to the owner as close as possible to the door of the aircraft, or at the baggage claim area, according to the passenger's request before boarding. If the priority storage for mobility aids prevents another passenger's baggage from being carried, the carrier shall make its best efforts to ensure the other baggage arrives within four hours.

On certain aircraft, assistive devices that are too large to fit in the cabin or in the cargo hold in one piece must be disassembled to be transported. When assistive devices are disassembled, carriers are obligated to return them to passengers in an assembled condition. In addition, carriers must allow passengers to provide written instructions concerning the disassembly and assembly of their wheelchairs.

Electric Wheelchairs

Carriers must transport battery-powered wheelchairs, unless cargo compartment size or aircraft airworthiness considerations do not permit doing so. However, carriers may require passengers with electric wheelchairs to check in one hour before flight time. If a passenger checks in less than one hour before flight time, the carrier must make a reasonable effort to carry the passenger's wheelchair unless this would delay the flight.

Electric wheelchairs must be treated in accordance with both DOT regulations for handling hazardous materials, and DOT Air Carrier Access regulations, which differentiate between spillable and non-spillable batteries, as set forth below.

If the wheelchair is powered by a spillable battery, the battery must be removed unless the wheelchair can be loaded, stored, secured and unloaded in an upright position at all times. If so, the carrier may not remove the battery from the chair. If the battery must be removed, the carrier may not charge for packaging wheelchair batteries. In addition, a wheelchair battery may not be drained.

It is never necessary under the DOT hazardous materials regulations to remove a battery that is marked as non-spillable from a wheelchair before stowing it. However, a non-spillable battery may be removed where it appears to be damaged and leakage of battery fluid is possible.

Liability for Damage or Loss

Carriers cannot require a passenger with a disability to sign a waiver of liability for damage or loss of wheelchairs or other assistive devices. The carrier may, however, make note of any pre-existing defect to the device.

On domestic trips, airlines are permitted to limit their liability for loss, damage or delay to checked baggage to $3,000 per passenger. However, this limit does not apply to wheelchairs or other assistive devices. When an assistive device is lost or destroyed on a domestic trip, the compensation allowed is the original purchase price of the device.

This expanded liability for assistive devices does not extend to international trips, where the Montreal Convention usually applies. For most international trips, including the domestic portions of an international trip, the liability is 1,000 Special Drawing Rights (SDR). Special Drawing Rights are discussed in Chapter 1, "Common Carriers," of this Almanac.

RIGHT TO ASSISTANCE IN BOARDING AND DEPLANING

Properly trained service personnel who are knowledgeable on how to assist disabled individuals in boarding and exiting the airplane must be available if needed, and the equipment used for assisting passengers must be kept in good working condition.

Boarding and exiting most medium and large-size jet aircraft is almost always by way of level boarding ramps or mobile lounges, which must be accessible. If ramps or mobile lounges are not used, a lifting device must be provided to assist persons with limited mobility safely on and off most flights using aircraft with 19 or more seats.

On smaller aircraft, passengers with mobility impairments are generally carried up and down the aircraft's boarding stairs using a "boarding chair." Airlines are not permitted to hand-carry passengers on and off aircraft, i.e., to directly pick a passenger's body in the arms of airline personnel.

In order to provide some personal assistance and extra time, the air carrier may offer a passenger with a disability, or any passenger that may be in need of assistance, the opportunity to pre-board the aircraft. The passenger has the option to accept or decline the offer.

On connecting flights, the original carrier is responsible for providing assistance to the disabled individual in reaching his or her connecting flight. Carriers cannot leave a passenger unattended for more than 30 minutes in a ground wheelchair, boarding chair or other device in which the passenger is not independently mobile.

RIGHT TO ACCESSIBLE SEATING

Pursuant to the Air Carrier Access rules, aircraft delivered after April 1992, and aircraft delivered before April 1992 that are undergoing refurbishment of their interior, must have accessible seating as set forth below.

Aircraft with 30 or More Passenger Seats

For aircraft with 30 ore more passenger seats:

1. at least one half of the armrests on aisle seats must be movable to facilitate transferring passengers from on-board wheelchairs to the aisle seat;

2. carriers must establish procedures to ensure that individuals with disabilities can readily obtain seating in rows with movable aisle armrests;

3. an aisle seat is not required to have a movable armrest if it is not feasible, or if a person with a disability would be precluded from sitting there by FAA safety rules, e.g., in an exit row, as discussed below.

Aircraft with 60 or More Passenger Seats

Aircraft with 60 or more passenger seats must have an operable on-board wheelchair if:

1. there is an accessible lavatory; or

2. a passenger provides advance notice that he or she can use an inaccessible lavatory but needs an on-board wheelchair to reach it. This rule applies even if the aircraft predated the rule and has not been refurbished.

Aircraft with 100 or More Passenger Seats

Aircraft with 100 or more passenger seats must provide priority space in the cabin for stowage of at least one passenger's folding wheelchair.

Aircraft with More Than One Aisle

Aircraft with more than one aisle must have at least one accessible lavatory with sufficient room to allow a passenger using an on-board wheelchair to enter, maneuver and use the facilities with the same degree of privacy as other passengers.

SEAT ASSIGNMENTS

An individual with a disability cannot be required to sit in a particular seat or be excluded from any seat, except as provided by FAA safety rules, such as the FAA exit row seating rule. For safety reasons, that rule limits seating in exit rows to those persons with the most potential to be able to operate the emergency exit and help in an aircraft evacuation.

In addition, the carrier cannot deny transport, but may deny specific seats to travelers who are less than age 15 or lack the capacity to act without an adult, or who lack sufficient mobility, strength, dexterity, vision, hearing, speech, reading or comprehension abilities to perform emergency evacuation functions.

The carrier may also deny specific seats to persons with a condition or responsibilities, such as caring for small children, which might prevent the person from performing emergency evacuation functions.

A traveler with a disability may also be denied certain seats if:

1. the passenger's involuntary behavior is such that it could compromise the safety of the flight, and the safety problem can be mitigated to an acceptable degree by assigning the passenger a specific seat rather than refusing service; or

2. the seat desired cannot accommodate guide dogs or service animals.

In each instance, carriers are obligated to offer alternative seat locations.

RIGHT TO BRING SERVICE ANIMALS ON BOARD

The U.S. Department of Transportation requires carriers to permit guide dogs or other service animals to accompany an individual with a disability on a flight. This is so even if the airline has a policy against allowing pets to travel in the passenger cabins. Service animals are not considered pets. There is no limit to the number of service animals that can be on any flight.

The service animal must have appropriate identification. Identification may include cards or other documentation, presence of a harness or markings on a harness, tags or the credible verbal assurance of the passenger using the animal. Unlike pets, service animals do not need any health certificates to travel, and do not need to be confined in a container or cage.

Carriers must permit a service animal to accompany a traveler with a disability to any seat in which the person sits, unless the animal obstructs an aisle or other area that must remain clear in order to facilitate an emergency evacuation. If so, the passenger will be assigned another seat.

If carriers provide special information to passengers concerning the transportation of animals outside the continental United States, they must provide such information to all passengers with animals on such flights, not simply to passengers with disabilities who are traveling with service animals.

RIGHT TO ASSISTANCE DURING FLIGHT

Passengers with a disability have the right to assistance during the flight. For example, air carrier personnel must assist a passenger with a disability to:

1. move to and from seats as a part of the boarding and exiting process;

2. open packages and identify food, however, assistance with actual eating is not required;

3. use an on-board wheelchair when available to enable the passenger to move to and from the lavatory;

4. move to and from the lavatory, in the case of a semi-ambulatory person;

5. load and retrieve carry-on items, including mobility aids and other assistive devices stowed on board the aircraft.

Air carrier personnel are not required to perform medical services for an individual with a disability.

PROHIBITION AGAINST CHARGING FOR ACCOMMODATIONS

Carriers cannot impose charges for providing facilities, equipment or services to an individual with a disability that are required by DOT's Air Carrier Access regulations. They may charge for optional services, however, such as oxygen and accommodation of stretchers.

PERSONNEL TRAINING REQUIREMENT

Carriers must provide training concerning passengers with disabilities for all personnel who deal with the traveling public. This training must be appropriate to the duties of each employee and will be designed to help the employee understand the special needs of these travelers, and how they can be accommodated quickly, safely, and with dignity. The training must familiarize employees with:

1. the Department of Transportation's rules on the provision of air service to an individual with a disability;

2. the carrier's procedures for providing transportation to persons with disabilities, including the proper and safe operation of any equipment used to accommodate such persons;

3. how to respond appropriately to persons with different disabilities, including persons with mobility, sensory, mental, and emotional disabilities.

RESOLVING DISPUTES

Under the DOT rules, new procedures were established for resolving disputes between the air carrier and its passengers:

1. All air carriers are now required to have a Complaints Resolution Official (CRO) immediately available to resolve disagreements that may arise between the air carrier and passengers with disabilities.

2. Travelers who disagree with a carrier's actions toward them can pursue the issue with the carrier's CRO on the spot. The CRO, however, does not have authority to countermand a safety-based decision made by the pilot-in-command of an aircraft.

3. If the CRO agrees with the passenger that a violation of the rule occurred, he must provide the passenger with a written statement summarizing the facts and what steps if any, the carrier proposes to take in response to the violation.

4. If the CRO determines that no violation has occurred, he must provide the passenger a written statement summarizing the facts and reasons for the decision or conclusion.

5. The written statement must inform the passenger of his or her right to pursue DOT enforcement action if the passenger is still not satisfied with the response. If possible, the written statement by the CRO must be given to the passenger at the airport; otherwise, it must be sent to the passenger within 10 days of the incident.

6. Carriers are required to establish a procedure for resolving written complaints alleging violations of any of the Air Carrier Access rules. If a passenger chooses to file a written complaint, the complaint

must note whether the passenger contacted the CRO at the time of the alleged violation, including the CRO's name and the date of contact, if available. The complaint should also include any written response received from the CRO. Nevertheless, the carrier is not required to respond to a complaint postmarked more than 45 days after the date of the alleged violation.

7. The carrier must respond to a written complaint within 30 days after receiving it. The response must state the airline's position concerning the alleged violation, and may also state whether and why no violation occurred, or what the airline plans to do about the problem. The carrier must also inform the passenger of his or her right to pursue DOT enforcement action.

8. If the passenger is still not satisfied with the way the dispute is being handled, he or she may pursue DOT enforcement action.

A complaint may be filed with the Department of Transportation online or by mail, as follows:

> Department of Transportation
> Aviation Consumer Protection
> Division, C-75
> 1200 New Jersey Ave., S.E.
> Washington, D.C. 20590
> Website: http://airconsumer.ost.dot.gov/escomplaint/es.cfm

ANNUAL REPORT REQUIREMENT ON DISABILITY-RELATED COMPLAINTS

On April 5, 2000, the Wendell H. Ford Aviation Investment and Reform Act for the 21st Century (AIR-21—Public Law 106-181) was enacted. AIR-21 requires, among other things, that the Secretary of Transportation: (1) regularly review all of the disability discrimination complaints received by air carriers; and (2) report annually to Congress on the results of the review.

On July 8, 2003, the U.S. Department of Transportation published a final rule to implement the requirements of AIR-21. The rule applies to certified U.S. air carriers and foreign air carriers operating to, from or within the United States, conducting passenger operations with at least one aircraft having a seating capacity of more than 60 passengers. Under the rule, the air carriers are required to record all complaints they receive alleging discrimination or inadequate accessibility on the basis of a disability.

The complaints are categorized according to the passenger's type of disability and the nature of the complaint.

Complaint Categories

The passenger's disability must be recorded as one of the following types:

1. Vision Impaired

2. Hearing Impaired

3. Vision and Hearing Impaired

4. Mentally Impaired

5. Communicable Disease

6. Allergic (e.g., food allergies, chemical sensitivity)

7. Paraplegic

8. Quadriplegic

9. Other Wheelchair

10. Oxygen

11. Stretcher

12. Other Assistive Device (cane, respirator, etc.)

13. Other Disability

Nature of the Complaint

The nature of the alleged discrimination or service problem related to the disability must be recorded in the following categories:

1. Refusal to Board

2. Refusal to Board without an Attendant

3. Security Issues Concerning Disability

4. Aircraft Not Accessible

5. Airport Not Accessible

6. Advance-Notice Dispute

7. Seating Accommodation

8. Failure to Provide Adequate or Timely Assistance

9. Damage to Assistive Device

10. Storage or Delay of Assistive Device

11. Service Animal Problem

12. Unsatisfactory Information

13. Other Complaint

The air carriers covered by the rule are also required to retain copies of the complaints and records of action taken for each complaint for 3 years, and to submit the required disability-related complaint data to the DOT annually.

2007 Annual Report

The most recent report released in 2007 is based on data for the 2006 calendar year. The 55 U.S. carriers that submitted data reported receiving 12,075 disability-related air travel complaints, and the 106 foreign air carriers reported receiving 1,691 complaints during this time period. More than half of the complaints reported (6,797) concerned the failure to provide adequate assistance to persons using wheelchairs.

CHAPTER 4:
RAILROADS

THE FEDERAL RAILROAD ADMINISTRATION

The Federal Railroad Administration (FRA) was created by Congress pursuant to the Department of Transportation Act of 1966. The FRA is responsible for:

1. promulgating and enforcing rail safety regulations;

2. administering railroad assistance programs;

3. conducting research and development in support of improved railroad safety and national rail transportation policy;

4. providing for the rehabilitation of Northeast Corridor rail passenger service; and

5. consolidating government support of rail transportation activities.

The FRA is made up of seven divisions, as set forth below.

Office of Financial Management and Administration

The Office of Financial Management and Administration directs and coordinates the administrative programs and services of the FRA.

Office of Chief Counsel

The Office of Chief Counsel provides legal services to FRA's various offices on all legal issues other than safety law. The Safety Law Division develops and drafts the agency's safety regulations, assesses civil penalties for violations of the rail safety statutes and FRA safety regulations, and provides other legal support for the FRA's safety program.

Office of Civil Rights

The Office of Civil Rights is responsible for civil rights compliance and monitoring to ensure non-discrimination in passenger railroad services.

Office of Policy

The Office of Policy provides support, analysis and recommendations on broad subjects relating to the railroad industry.

Office of Public Affairs

The Office of Public Affairs works closely with all departments within the agency in developing timely information for release through a variety of print and electronic news outlets as well as distribution to the general public.

Office of Railroad Development

The Office of Railroad Development is responsible for federal investment and assistance to the rail industry as well as the development and implementation of Administration policy concerning intercity rail passenger service and high-speed rail.

Office of Safety

The Office of Safety promotes and regulates safety throughout the nation's railroad industry.

THE NATIONAL RAILROAD PASSENGER CORPORATION (AMTRAK)

Intercity Rail Service

The National Railroad Passenger Corporation, commonly known as Amtrak, was created by Congress pursuant to the Rail Passenger Service Act of 1970. Amtrak operates all long-distance intercity rail services in the United States. Intercity rail services are express train passenger services that travel longer distances than commuter trains. Amtrak trains operate in 46 states and the District of Columbia.

Amtrak's Board of Directors consists of 7 voting members who are appointed for five-year terms by the President, including the Secretary of Transportation. The board is responsible for managing the company and setting policy.

High Speed Ground Transportation

High Speed Ground Transportation (HSGT) refers to intercity passenger ground transportation that is time-competitive with air transportation and automobiles for trips in the range of 100 to 500 miles. HSGT provides a viable alternative to both air transportation and automobiles. HSGT benefits the long-term growth in America's population, income, travel demand, and congestion in intercity transportation by air and automobiles.

HSGT is designed to address long-term passenger transportation needs in heavily populated corridors. A "corridor" is a natural grouping of metropolitan areas and markets that, by their proximity and configuration, lend themselves to efficient service by ground transportation, such as the Northeast Corridor, which includes Washington, New York and Boston.

Governing Law

All travel on Amtrak and related transactions is governed by the laws of the District of Columbia. Passengers who travel on Amtrak agree to submit to the exclusive jurisdiction of any state or federal court located in the District of Columbia, and waive any jurisdictional, venue or inconvenient forum objections to such courts.

Reservations

Reservations to travel on Amtrak must be made when required, and tickets are not transferable. Amtrak reserves the right to refuse passengers who:

1. have not paid the applicable fare;

2. engage in objectionable conduct, such as, but not limited to, being under the influence of alcohol or narcotics;

3. pose a health, safety or security hazard to other passengers or employees, or whose personal hygiene makes them offensive;

4. refuse to comply with safety or security rules, or with instructions of Amtrak personnel;

5. would require Amtrak personnel to provide personal care services, or otherwise do not meet the essential requirements for travel on Amtrak; or

6. refuse to consent to Amtrak security inspections of persons or their baggage onboard Amtrak trains or other designated areas, such as train platforms and passenger boarding or waiting areas.

Seating Policies

Passenger seating must comply with the following Amtrak policies:

1. Each passenger paying a fare will be entitled to a seat, to the extent coach seats are available.

2. Passengers are entitled to one seat per fare, to ensure other paying passengers are not excluded.

3. Unless specific seats are assigned, seating is on a first come/first served basis. On unreserved trains there are no guaranteed seats.

4. Seating arrangements will be made without regard to race, color, gender, creed or national origin.

5. Amtrak reserves the right, whenever operating conditions require, to transfer passengers from one car or train to another.

6. Children under the age of 2, who are traveling free, may occupy a vacant seat only if it is not yet needed for a paying passenger. The conductor may request that such a child be removed from the seat for a fare-paying passenger, unless the passenger traveling with the child opts to purchase a ticket for the child.

Fares

Amtrak will quote and price your travel at the lowest fare available at the time you make your reservation, as follows:

1. On reserved trains, a range of fares may apply, the lower of which are more widely available at certain times of the year.

2. On unreserved trains, the lowest fares may be restricted during peak travel periods.

3. Changes to your itinerary may affect the fare, and a fee may apply when tickets are reissued.

4. Some discount fares may require purchase in advance of travel, and are non-refundable.

5. Certain fares are subject to significant cancellation penalties.

Ticketing

All passengers purchasing tickets from station ticket agents or on board trains from conductors must be at least 15 years old and provide valid photo identification. Passengers are advised to purchase their tickets prior to boarding the train if the passenger boards at any staffed station, or a station equipped with a Quik-Trak kiosk. Tickets purchased on board include a service fee that cannot be waived.

Your ticket is evidence that you paid your fare. The ticket sets forth the type of ticket you purchased and any conditions or limitations. A ticket is valid between the stations listed on the ticket, for the class of service and accommodations listed, and during the time period stated on the ticket.

A ticket is void if it bears any alterations or erasures, or if the passenger receipt is detached. In addition, a ticket must not be used by any person other than the individual for whom it was originally purchased, unless authorized by fare code rules.

Tickets must be surrendered for cancellation or inspection by any conductor or authorized representative.

Unaccompanied Minors

Children age 15 and older may travel unaccompanied, and are subject to all of the policies that apply to adult passengers. Children age 15 and older may purchase tickets on their own from a ticket agent or conductor if they present valid photo identification.

Children ages 8 to 14 may travel unaccompanied subject to the following restrictions:

1. Travel is permitted on Amtrak trains only.

2. The scheduled departure time may be no earlier than 6AM, and arrival time no later than 9PM.

3. No transfers of any kind are permitted.

4. The boarding and arrival stations must be staffed.

5. An adult age 18 years or older must bring the child who will be traveling alone to the station at least one hour prior to departure time to allow for the required interview, and to complete necessary forms. The adult must produce valid current identification, and must complete and sign a release form, and must remain at the station until the train has departed.

6. The child must be interviewed to determine whether he or she is capable of traveling alone.

7. The child must wear an Amtrak issued wristband for the duration of travel.

8. An adult age 18 years or older must be present to pick up the child upon arrival. The adult must produce valid current identification.

9. The full adult fares will be charged.

10. An unaccompanied child may not travel if he or she has any life-threatening food allergies.

Children age 7 years old and younger may not travel alone, but must be accompanied by a person who is age 15 or older, who has responsibility for the child.

Ticket Refunds

Passengers who do not use their ticket, or make partial use of their ticket, are entitled to a refund, subject to certain limitations. In addition, if a ticket is purchased in advance, it is subject to the same refund policies set forth below, even if the ticket has not yet been printed.

Merely canceling or changing your reservation does not generate your refund. Unless you purchased your ticket in advance and have not yet received a printed ticket, you must produce the actual, original, unused or partially used ticket in order to obtain a refund.

Refund Calculation

Before you can claim a ticket refund, the value of your refund must be calculated. Refunds are calculated separately on each component of the total charges paid, as set forth below:

Rail Fare

Most rail fare tickets are refundable before travel begins. In most cases, partially used regular, full-fare and one-way tickets may be returned for a partial refund. Some discount tickets are non-refundable once the ticket has been purchased.

Passengers who downgrade accommodations or reduce the number in their party on board trains must obtain a Refund Authorization Form from the conductor.

First Class/Business Class Charge

First class seat charges on Acela Express trains, and business class seat charges on other trains, are refundable if reservations are can-celled at least one hour prior to departure. If not, the seat charge amount will not be refundable but it may be applied to future Amtrak travel purchases. However, this penalty will not be imposed if the customer cancels travel because the train is one hour or more late at the boarding station.

Sleeping Car Accommodation Charge

The sleeping car accommodation charge is refundable if the sleeping car reservation is cancelled at least seven days prior to departure. If the reservation is cancelled less than seven days prior to departure, but before actual departure, the accommodation charge is not refundable but may be applied to future travel purchases. The passenger will be issued a non-refundable exchange voucher.

If the reservation is not cancelled before actual departure, the accom-modation charge is neither refundable nor may it be applied to future travel. However, this penalty will not be imposed if the customer can-cels travel because the train is two hours or more late at the boarding station.

Vehicle Accommodation Charge

The vehicle accommodation charge, which applies to automobiles, vans, motorcycles, and bicycles, is refundable at any time.

Refund Options

Once the value of a refund has been determined, as set forth above, passengers have two options on how to receive the refund:

1. passengers may receive the full calculated refund value in the form of a non-refundable exchange voucher valid for future travel purchases; or

2. passengers may receive the calculated refund value, in the form of cash, check or credit card refund, depending on the form of payment that was used for the ticket being refunded. If the passenger selects this option, there will be a 10% refund service charge deducted from the refund amount, up to a maximum of $100 per reservation.

Time Limitation

An Amtrak ticket becomes non-refundable, not valid for travel, and has no exchange value after one year from the date the ticket is issued. An exchange voucher is valid for one year from the date it is issued, which may be renewed prior to the voucher's expiration date.

Applying for the Refund

Most refunds can be processed at an Amtrak ticket office, depending on the type of ticket and the form of payment. Tickets purchased at a travel agency must be returned to that agency; however, Amtrak will process travel agency ticket refunds caused by a downgrade or a service disruption.

Most tickets purchased online can be cancelled and refunded online. However, if you made modifications to your trip after booking it online, you cannot cancel online.

Amtrak can process your unused ticket refund by mail. Send original tickets using certified mail with a return receipt requested to:

Amtrak Customer Refunds
P.O. Box 70 - 30th St. Station
2955 Market Street
Philadelphia, PA 19104-2898

Lost, Stolen or Destroyed Tickets

Tickets have value; therefore, they should be safeguarded. Amtrak will not be liable for lost, stolen, misplaced or destroyed tickets. If you lose your ticket, you will have to repurchase another ticket in order to travel.

You may apply for a refund for a lost or destroyed ticket by submitting a Lost Ticket Refund Application to Amtrak, however, not all tickets are eligible for refund. You must submit the application within one year from the purchase date.

In addition, you must provide a ticket number for the lost ticket; therefore, it is advisable to write down your ticket number upon purchasing it. Applications for refunds for lost tickets are held for five months from the date received before processing.

A sample Lost Ticket Refund Application can be found in Appendix 8 of this Almanac.

Passengers with Disabilities

Reservations

Passengers with disabilities must make their reservation for special accommodations, e.g., wheelchair space, accessible sleeper accommodations, etc. Since space is limited, reservations should be made as far in advance of travel as possible.

Reservations for such accommodations must be made even if the train is an "unreserved" train, i.e., a train that does not ordinarily require a reservation, as accessible space is limited.

Up until 14 days prior to departure, reservations for accessible bedrooms may only be made for passengers who are mobility impaired. After this period, if all other deluxe and family bedrooms have been reserved, accessible bedrooms are made available to all passengers on a first-come/first-served basis.

Discounts

Amtrak offers a rail fare discount to passengers with disabilities. To receive the discount, you must book your reservation by telephone or at a ticket counter. In addition, you must provide written documentation of your disability at the ticket counter and when boarding the train.

Acceptable documentation includes:

1. a transit system ID card;

2. a membership card from a disabilities organization; or

3. a letter from a physician.

You may not combine this discount with any other discount program.

Ticketing

If you purchase your ticket at least one week prior to departure, Amtrak will mail your ticket to you. If you are departing from a station with a staffed and open ticket office, you may pick up your ticket when you arrive at the station.

Travel Assistance

If you require assistance at the station, you should make this request when you book your reservation. Amtrak personnel at staffed stations will provide assistance to and from the restrooms, or help with stairs.

Wheelchairs

Courtesy wheelchairs and wheelchair lifts are available at most Amtrak staffed stations. Amtrak personnel will provide wheelchair assistance in the following situations, if necessary:

1. Amtrak will assist you across the gap between the platform and the train by using a bridge plate.

2. Amtrak will provide a level boarding through the use of station-board lifts.

3. Amtrak will provide a wheelchair ramp to help you board the lower level of a bi-level train.

Amtrak trains can accommodate most manually operated and battery powered wheelchairs. However, the dimensions of the wheelchair must not exceed 30 inches in width, 48 inches in length and 2 inches of ground clearance. The weight of an occupied wheelchair must not exceed 600 pounds.

Oxygen

Transporting oxygen onboard the train is prohibited unless a passenger requires supplemental oxygen for medical reasons. If you need to bring oxygen onboard, you must make reservations in advance. Amtrak requires at least 12 hours advance notice prior to boarding of your need to bring oxygen aboard.

Portable oxygen containers must meet the following requirements:

1. Oxygen equipment must have its own power source and be able to operate a minimum of four hours without available onboard electrical power.

2. Oxygen equipment must be Underwriter's Laboratory (UL) or Factory Mutual (FM) listed.

3. Each oxygen tank and its associated equipment may weigh no more than 50 lbs.

4. The oxygen tank must be either: (a) a two-tank system weighing a maximum of 50 lbs per tank; or (b) a six-tank system weighing a maximum of 20 lbs per tank, if the tanks can be separated and handled individually.

Service Animals

Amtrak allows trained service animals to accompany passengers with disabilities in all customer areas in Amtrak stations, trains and on Amtrak Thruway motor coaches. Trained service animals must be kept under the control of their owners or trainers at all times. No other animals are permitted onboard at any time.

The service animal must be kept under control at all times and comply with local animal safety regulations. The animal must be kept on a leash or in a carrier, except as required for boarding or detraining. If the animal causes a disturbance, train employees have the right to remove the animal from the train and turn it over to local animal control officials.

Security Measures

In order to protect its passengers, Amtrak has instituted security measures, including those listed below.

Photo ID Requirement

Passengers over the age of 18 are required to produce valid photo identification under the following circumstances:

1. purchasing, exchanging, and refunding tickets;

2. storing baggage at stations;

3. checking baggage;

4. sending Amtrak Express shipments; and

5. onboard trains, in response to a request by an Amtrak employee.

This requirement also applies to unaccompanied children age 15 and older when purchasing tickets.

To be valid, your identification must be current and in-force. The following forms of identification are acceptable for persons 18 and older:

1. one piece of photo identification issued by a government authority; or

2. two pieces of identification, at least one of which is a non-photo ID issued by a government authority.

Examples of acceptable forms of identification include:

1. state or Canadian provincial driver's license;

2. passport;

3. official government-issued identification, including federal, state or county government identification, or legitimate foreign government identification;

4. Canadian provincial health card ID card with photo;

5. military photo ID;

6. student identification, including university, college or high school photo identification; and

7. Job Corps photo ID.

Random Onboard Ticket/ID Checks

Pursuant to federal Transportation Security Administration (TSA) guidelines, Amtrak regularly conducts random ticket verification checks onboard trains to ensure that passengers are properly ticketed. In addition, a passenger must show valid photo identification upon the request of an Amtrak employee.

Random Searches

The security measures implemented by Amtrak include the placement of uniformed police officers, mobile security teams and K-9 units located onboard Amtrak trains, or in the Amtrak stations. Randomly selected passengers and their baggage, and personal items may be screened or inspected.

If you refuse to submit to these security procedures, you will not be allowed to travel. Under these circumstances, you may request a refund for your ticket.

Baggage Handling

Carry-On Luggage

Amtrak limits the amount of baggage you may carry onboard to two pieces of luggage. This does not include briefcases, purses and laptops, or similar items. Each piece of luggage cannot weigh more than 50 pounds, and cannot exceed 28×22×14 inches in size. All luggage must have identification tags with your name and address visibly attached to the luggage.

Checked Luggage

Checked luggage is limited to three pieces of luggage weighing no more than 50 pounds each. Checked bags cannot exceed 36×36×36 inches in size. You may check three additional pieces of luggage for an extra charge. Baggage must be checked in at least 30 minutes before departure or risk being delayed. You must show a valid photo ID when you check your bags.

At check-in, you will receive a claim check for your luggage. Checked luggage will be available approximately 30 minutes after arrival at the destination. You must present your claim check to retrieve your checked luggage. If you fail to claim your luggage within two days of arrival, you will be charged a fee for storage.

Prohibited Items

The following kinds of items are prohibited as both checked and carry-on baggage:

1. any type of gun, firearm, ammunition, explosives or weapon;

2. incendiaries, including flammable gases, liquids and fuels;

3. large, sharp objects such as axes, ice picks and swords;

4. corrosive or dangerous chemicals or materials, such as liquid bleach, tear gas, mace, radioactive and harmful bacteriological materials;

5. batteries with acid that can spill or leak, except for batteries used in motorized wheelchairs or similar devices for mobility-impaired passengers;

6. club-like items, such as billy clubs and nightsticks;

7. fragile and/or valuable items, including but not limited to electronic equipment. Laptop computers and handheld devices may be carried onboard, however, Amtrak will not be liable for or damage to such items;

8. animals, except service animals;

9. oversized and/or overweight items; and

10. any item similar to those listed above.

Bicycles

Many Amtrak trains permit passengers to bring their bicycles. Space for bicycles onboard is limited and not available on all trains, so it is advisable to check first before bringing your bicycles. You can call 1-800-USA-RAIL to determine whether bicycle storage space is available on a particular train and route.

The following bicycle storage options may be available, depending on the train:

Bicycles Stored Onboard

On some Amtrak trains you can secure your bicycle in a bicycle rack. This service varies widely from train to train, and station to station. Bicycle racks cannot hold unusual bicycles, such as tandem or recumbent bikes. Such bicycles must be checked in a box.

You can reserve rack space for bicycles when you make a ticket reservation. Amtrak charges a fee for reserving a space in the bike rack. If space is available, you will be issued a ticket for bike rack space, which you must present to the conductor when boarding.

Amtrak disclaims liability for loss of or damage to bicycles carried onboard and stored in bike racks.

Folding bicycles may be brought aboard certain passenger cars as carry-on baggage. Generally, these bicycles have small wheels and frame latches that allow the frame to be collapsed. You must fold up your folding bicycle before boarding the train and store it in the luggage storage areas at the end of the car. You may not store folding bicycles in overhead racks.

Bicycles as Checked Baggage

You can bring your bicycle on Amtrak as checked baggage between all cities where checked baggage services are offered. If you wish to check your bicycle in storage, you should arrive at least one hour before departure. Bicycles must be transported in a bicycle box, which may be available at certain train stations. Generally, bicycles must be partially disassembled to fit in the box. You must place your name and address on the box.

Some trains have tie-down equipment in the baggage car or other areas designated for checked baggage. When such equipment is available, you can check your bike without a box. Since space is limited, you must reserve space for a fee. Further, you must accompany an unboxed bike on the same train. Unboxed bicycles are more likely to be damaged in transit. Thus Amtrak disclaims liability for loss or damage to unboxed bicycles.

Lost or Damaged Luggage

Amtrak disclaims liability for carry-on baggage, even if Amtrak personnel has handled or assisted in loading or unloading the baggage.

Claims for lost checked baggage must be submitted within 30 days of arrival at your destination station. Claims for damaged or delayed checked baggage, or for a concealed loss within checked baggage, must be submitted immediately at your destination station. Amtrak disclaims liability for a concealed loss in an unsecured bag, such as a bag that does not have a lock or device that protects the bag from being opened, and for articles placed in an unlocked or unsecured exterior baggage compartment.

Amtrak liability for checked baggage is limited to a maximum of $500 per ticketed passenger. Passengers may declare additional valuation up to $2,500 for a fee.

Traveling Across U.S./Canadian Border

There are certain requirements you must abide by if you will be traveling across the U.S./Canadian border, as set forth below.

Reservations

When making a reservation for travel across the U.S./Canadian border, you must provide certain detailed information including: date of birth; gender; country of citizenship; and the form of identification you will use during travel. This information is entered into your reservation record and forwarded to Customs and Immigration officers.

It is important that you comply with this requirement and supply any additional information requested. If you do not provide accurate and complete information, you may be delayed while the authorities conduct an extensive inspection and questioning at the border crossing.

Required Identification

Amtrak trains that cross the U.S./Canadian border must comply with any inspection requested by Canadian or American law enforcement officials. As part of this inspection, passengers may be required to show proof of citizenship and proof of identity.

You should be prepared to show the same identification you provided information about when you made your reservation. The document must be the original and current. Photocopies or expired identification will not be accepted.

In addition, American and Canadian citizens are advised to bring their passport. If you do not have a passport, you must bring a certified copy of your birth certificate and a valid, current, government-issued photo identification. Citizens of all other countries are required to carry a valid passport, and may also be required to carry a visa.

Passengers who are under the age of 18, who are not traveling with both parents, must carry a notarized letter of permission to travel across the border signed, by the parent or legal guardian who is not traveling. The letter must include the non-traveling parent or legal guardian's address and telephone number. If one parent is deceased, a copy of that parent's death certificate will facilitate the process and mitigate any delay.

Children age 14 and under are not permitted to travel unaccompanied into Canada under any circumstances, even if they provide photo identification and a notarized letter of permission.

The US-VISIT Program

The US-VISIT Program is a border inspection program implemented by the U.S. Department of Homeland Security. Foreign visitors who are carrying a foreign passport and/or those visitors who are required to complete a form I-94 will be enrolled in the US-VISIT program at Amtrak border crossings.

For first-time visitors to the United States, a U.S. Customs and Border Protection Officer will use an inkless, digital finger scanner to perform a ten-finger finger scan. Subsequent entries and exits by the same person at air, sea and land border ports will require two-finger scans for verification.

In addition, a U.S. Customs and Border Protection Officer will take a digital picture of the visitor, review his or her travel documents and inquire about the visitor's stay in the United States. This process should take less than five minutes per passenger.

Entry into the United States or Canada is not guaranteed by Amtrak, and is solely at the discretion of Customs and Immigration officers. If you are denied entry or delayed at the border by Customs and Immigration officers, Amtrak disclaims any liability for such denial or delay. In addition, if you are detained at the border, Amtrak trains will proceed to their destination without delay.

There is a small fee for processing each visitor through the US-Visit Program. The fee is presently $6.00, payable in U.S. currency, or by U.S. postal money order; a personal check drawn on a U.S. bank; a Canadian money order issued in U.S. funds; or a traveler's check issued in U.S. funds.

RAPID TRANSIT SYSTEM

A rapid transit system, also referred to as a subway or metro system, is generally defined as an urban, electric passenger transportation system with high capacity and high frequency of service, which is totally independent from other traffic, roads or pedestrians.

The trains may operate underground, elevated or at surface level. The trains operate along designated lines between stations on a regular and frequent schedule. In general, rapid transit trains routes are shorter than commuter train routes.

Most rapid transit systems are government owned and operated. The government generally operates a corresponding bus service that offers passengers free transfer between the two modes of travel in order to reach a destination outside of the train route.

Transit maps that provide passengers with route information are generally located at stations and on the trains. In general, passengers do not need a schedule as rapid transit systems operate on a higher frequency basis, e.g., 5 to 10 minutes between trains.

Rules of Conduct

Because rapid transit systems often transport large numbers of passengers, many systems publish a rules of conduct that must be followed in order to maintain the safe and secure travel for passengers.

For example, the New York City Transit Authority (NYCTA) operates the New York City subway system, one of the largest and most intricate rapid transit systems in the world. According to the NYCTA rules of conduct, it is a violation to:

1. jump the turnstile or enter the system improperly, even if the passenger's MetroCard is not working properly;

2. refuse to present a special fare card to a police officer or transit employee;

3. straddle a bicycle, wear in-line or roller skates, stand on a skateboard or ride a scooter;

4. move between end doors of a subway car whether or not the train is in motion, except in an emergency, or when directed by a police officer or conductor;

5. place one's foot on the seat of a subway, bus, or platform bench; occupy more than one seat or place bags on an empty seat when doing so would interfere with transit operations or the comfort of other customers;

6. fail to pay the proper fare;

7. panhandle or beg;

8. play a radio audible to others or use amplified devices on platforms;

9. block free movement;

10. lie down;

11. drink alcoholic beverages;

12. carry any liquid in an open container;

13. engage in unauthorized commercial activity;

14. enter tracks, tunnels or other non-public areas;

15. carry bulky items likely to cause inconvenience or hazard;

16. damage subway or bus property;

17. litter or create unsanitary conditions; or

18. smoke anywhere on NYC Transit property, including outdoor stations.

Passengers with Disabilities

In general, rapid transit systems are required to take steps to make sure the system meets the needs of customers with disabilities. Under the Americans with Disabilities Act (ADA), these entities must make every effort to ensure their facilities are accessible for customers with visual, hearing, and mobility impairments. Accessibility features include:

1. elevators or ramps;

2. handrails on ramps and stairs;

3. large-print and tactile-Braille signs;

4. audio and visual information systems;

5. accessible station booth windows;

6. accessible vending machines to obtain fare cards;

7. accessible service entry gates at stations;

8. platform-edge warning strips;

9. platform gap modifications or bridge plates to reduce or eliminate the gap between trains and platforms;

10. telephones at an accessible height with volume control, and text telephones (TTYs); and

11. accessible restrooms at stations that have restrooms.

In addition, many rapid transit systems offer reduced fares to passengers with disabilities, and allow personal care assistants—i.e., persons employed to assist individuals with disabilities—to ride the system free when accompanying a person who is carrying identification that indicates such assistance is required.

Customers with disabilities are also permitted to bring their service animals into all transit facilities. However, the animals must be securely leashed for the safety of the other passengers.

Discrimination

Under Title VI of the Civil Rights Act, no person may be excluded from participation in, or denied the benefits of, or be subject to discrimination in the receipt of services on the basis of race, color or national origin. Passengers who believe they have been subjected to discrimination under Title VI may file a written complaint with the governmental authority that operates the particular rapid transit system.

A directory of rapid transit systems in the United States can be found in Appendix 9 of this Almanac.

COMMUTER RAIL SYSTEM

A commuter rail system, also referred to as suburban rail system, offers scheduled transportation to passengers who travel on a daily basis between a city center, where many are employed, and outer suburbs and towns, consisting of mostly residential areas. Unlike rapid transit systems, as discussed above, commuter rail trains travel according to a definite schedule.

Commuter trains travel distances of approximately 10 to 125 miles, and generally provide seating for all passengers. Commuter rail stations are located in areas that are not within walking distance of most passengers, thus automobile parking and taxi service is generally available at the station.

A directory of commuter rail systems in the United States can be found in Appendix 10 of this Almanac.

Accessibility and Discrimination

Commuter rail systems are subject to the same accessibility guidelines under the Americans with Disabilities Act as rapid transit systems, as set forth above. In addition, commuter rail systems are also prohibited from discriminating against passengers on the basis of race, color or national origin.

Highway and Rail Crossing Safety

Unlike rapid transit systems, which are totally independent from other traffic, roads or pedestrians, commuter trains often share a track with intercity and freight trains. With street-level crossings, the commuter rail tracks must necessarily interact with other traffic, roads and pedestrians.

A highway-railroad grade crossing is an intersection where a roadway crosses railroad tracks at the same level. There are more than 350,000 public and private highway-rail grade crossings in the United States.

Railroad crossings are extremely dangerous areas; therefore, pedestrians and vehicles must take extreme caution when approaching a crossing. According to the Federal Railroad Administration (FRA), there are approximately 900 deaths per year at highway-rail grade crossings and along railroad rights-of-way. In fact, over 90% of all deaths caused by accidents involving the railroad industry occur at railroad crossings.

The FRA advises pedestrians not to cross train tracks at locations other than public crossings. In addition, pedestrians should never attempt to cross the tracks when:

1. the gate is lowered, or being opened or closed;

2. there is an audible or visible electronic or mechanical signal device, or human flagman, warning of an approaching train; or

3. the pedestrian can hear or see a train approaching.

CHAPTER 5:
BUSES

IN GENERAL

A bus—also referred to as a "coach" or "motorcoach"—is generally defined as a large multi-seated vehicle that travels on land and is designed to carry a driver and numerous passengers along a designated route. In general, there are two categories of motor coach service, a long distance intercity coach service and an urban-suburban commuter bus line.

THE AMERICAN BUS ASSOCIATION

The American Bus Association (ABA) represents approximately 1,000 motorcoach and tour companies in the United States and Canada. Another 2,300 member organizations represent the travel and tourism industry.

ABA members operate charter, tour, regular route, airport express, special operations and contract services, including commuter, school and transit services. ABA members include motorcoach operators; tour operators; and the travel industry.

Motorcoach operators own motorcoaches and provide services such as charters, tours, sightseeing, scheduled service, school bus service, special operations and local operations.

Tour operators organize tours without owning equipment, and contract for coach and other transportation, for hotels, attractions and other travel suppliers to offer a package. The tours are primarily to locations away from the company's location.

The travel industry consists of tourism-related companies and organizations.

ABA Bus Industry Safety Council

Bus travel is the safest means of travel. Approximately 631 million passengers ride motorcoaches annually, and the industry's safety record of 0.02 fatalities per 100 million passenger miles traveled documents the safety of bus travel.

The mission of the ABA Bus Industry Safety Council is to develop and promote methods, materials, and procedures to improve motorcoach safety. The council is comprised of security, mechanical, safety, operational and maintenance leaders from ABA's bus operator and supplier membership. The group meets regularly to discuss issues and innovations in areas of safety, regulatory compliance, mechanics, technology and security.

Code of Ethics

The ABA has adopted a Code of Ethics for its members to promote and maintain the highest standards of intercity bus service and personal conduct among its members.

The American Bus Association (ABA) Code of Ethics can be found in Appendix 11 of this Almanac.

INTERCITY AND RURAL BUS SERVICE

The intercity bus industry is known as the backbone of the intercity transportation network. Intercity and rural bus services provide transportation between cities and towns within a state. This service enables people to live in one town, and travel to other towns and cities for work, shopping, entertainment and services. Intercity buses make fewer stops than local buses, but travel further distances. For many people living in rural areas, coach service is the only available mode of intercity transportation.

Because these buses generally travel greater distances, the type of vehicle used is a coach-type bus, for passenger comfort. A coach is generally air-conditioned and usually has reclining seats and toilet facilities. Because these buses do not take on and discharge passengers during a short run, these coaches usually have only one door and do not provide for standing room. Luggage is stored below the floor, and is accessible from outside panels.

According to the U.S. Department of Transportation, Bureau of Transportation Statistics, intercity bus transportation is the safest mode of transportation over cars, trucks, trains, planes and other commercial vehicles, and is generally less expensive than traveling by air or rail.

Prior to the 1960s, intercity bus service was a booming business. Even the smallest towns and rural areas had access to intercity bus routes. Each year, the average American traveled hundreds of miles on intercity buses.

However, the demand for intercity bus service declined drastically with the advent of interstate highways, discounted airline tickets and the increase in automobile ownership. Most of the passengers who continued to travel by bus did so because they could not afford other modes of transportation.

There has been a recent surge in bus travel, due in large part to the rising price of gasoline and traffic congestion, although the increase is most significant for those passengers traveling short and mid-range distances.

Intercity Travel Tips

According to the ABA, the following tips should be heeded when using intercity bus transportation:

1. Call early for fare and schedule information; note details and bring them with you for ticketing.

2. Buy tickets in advance, and purchase round-trip if possible, to avoid lines for the return trip.

3. Arrive at the terminal at least 60 minutes before departure. During peak times, if your bus fills quickly, it may depart early, as extra buses may be added to the schedule.

4. Ask about luggage restrictions; excess baggage can cost you and slow down loading and unloading.

5. Put identification both inside and outside of your luggage.

6. Let the bus company help you determine your best route. Most scheduled-service bus companies can arrange for interline connections with other carriers and get you to your end destination with one ticket.

7. You may wish to bring a light sweater for use inside the bus. If traveling a long distance, bringing a sweater, small pillow, lightweight blanket and snack is advisable.

8. Remember to be prepared in case of weather delays.

As discussed below, Greyhound Lines is the largest provider of intercity bus transportation in the United States.

URBAN-SUBURBAN BUS SERVICE

An urban-suburban bus service connects a suburban area with an urban area, and generally includes routes that cover a longer distance than local transit routes. The type of bus used on such a route may be a refitted school bus, minibus, or suburban coach. The suburban coach is usually a standard transit bus with some modifications. For example, it may be air conditioned, with reclining seats and overhead storage. However, because it is a commuter bus, it may offer standing room for passengers.

Urban-suburban buses may not run as frequently or have as many stops as local transit buses. Most of the stops would be at the beginning or end of the route. In addition, this service may only operate one-way, towards the urban area, in the morning, and the other way, towards the suburban area, in the afternoon.

COMMUTER BUS SERVICE

Commuter bus service—also referred to as "local transit"—generally operates within a city. Local bus service transports passengers along designated routes and stops at frequent scheduled intervals to pick up and drop off passengers at locations known as "bus stops."

Some local bus services offer express service, which is designed to provide faster service to its passengers, but provides for fewer stops along the route. Express buses may also charge a higher fare than regular buses.

A bus stop is a designated place where a public transport bus stops for the purpose of allowing passengers to board or leave a bus. The bus stop is usually located along a marked curb next to the road. Typically, a sign with the bus route number is located at the bus stop. There may also be a route map and timetable located at the bus stop, along with a toll-free telephone number for passengers to call and receive transportation information. The bus stop may also contain a three-sided bus shelter with a roof where passengers may stand or sit on a bench while awaiting the bus.

Local transit buses contain a fixed number of seats and standing area for passengers. These buses typically have two doors, one located in the front of the bus and one located in the middle of the bus, to provide for easy boarding and exiting the bus. The local transit bus does not provide storage space for luggage.

BUS RAPID TRANSIT

Bus Rapid Transit (BRT) is an enhanced bus system that operates on bus lanes or other transitways in order to combine the flexibility of buses with the efficiency of rail. By doing so, BRT operates at faster speeds, provides greater service reliability and increased customer convenience, and provides significantly better service than traditional bus service.

Bus Lanes

A "bus lane" is a lane on a highway or road that is restricted to bus travel. The purpose of the bus lane is to keep public transportation moving by avoiding traffic congestion. Generally, bus lanes are open to other high occupancy vehicles. A bus lane is usually created for roads that are generally congested, particularly at certain hours of the day.

In some cases, the bus lanes only operate during those times of day when traffic congestion is likely, such as during rush hour. In addition, the bus lane may only operate in one direction, depending on the flow of traffic, e.g., the primary direction vehicles travel for the morning rush hour and evening rush hour.

SCHOOL BUS SERVICE

Every school day, some 450,000 yellow school buses transport more than 24 million children to and from schools and school-related activities. School buses provide approximately 10 billion student trips per year, including 8.8 billion children to and from school, and approximately 1.2 billion for trips, special events and athletic competitions.

According to the Transportation Research Board of the National Academy of Sciences, the school bus is the safest way for a student to travel to and from school. National Highway Traffic Safety Administration (NHTSA) statistics demonstrate that students are nearly eight times safer riding in a school bus than with their own parents in cars. The fatality rate for school buses is only 0.2 fatalities per 100 million miles traveled compared to 1.5 fatalities per 100 million miles traveled by car.

Required Safety Equipment

Modern school buses are equipped with more safety equipment than any other vehicle. In addition, the size of the school bus alone provides an important safety advantage. School buses are subject to the standards and regulations set forth by the U.S. Department of Transportation. Federal safety requirements include:

1. well-padded, high-back, energy-absorbing seats, as well as special requirements for wheelchair restraint systems. These seating systems provide "automatic protection" for young passengers. Additionally, school bus interiors are designed to reduce the chances of injury caused by sharp edges or body panels that may tear loose in a crash;

2. brake systems that enable the school bus to stop in a shorter distance than other large vehicles;

3. warning lights and reflective devices that indicate when the bus is loading and unloading passengers;

4. special mirrors that allow the driver to see all critical areas directly in front of and along both sides of the school bus;

5. a stop arm that extends out to the left side of the bus to warn motorists when the bus is loading or unloading passengers;

6. several emergency exits, based on the capacity of the school bus;

7. rollover protection that reduces the likelihood of a roof collapse and allows for operable emergency exits even after the roof is subject to extreme forces; and

8. protected fuel tanks, fuel pump, fuel delivery system, emissions control lines and connections to protect against fuel spills in severe crashes.

Seating Capacity and Occupant Protection

Federal regulation does not specify the number of persons that can sit on a school bus seat. The school bus manufacturers determine the maximum seating capacity of a school bus. School transportation providers generally determine the number of persons that they can safely fit into a school bus seat. Generally, they fit three smaller elementary school age children or two high school age children into a typical 39-inch school bus seat.

The NHTSA recommends that all passengers be seated entirely within the confines of the school bus seats while the bus is in motion. Federal motor vehicle safety standards require that the interior of large buses provide occupant protection so that children are protected without the need to buckle-up. Occupant crash protection is provided by closely-spaced seats with energy-absorbing seat backs. Children who are not sitting, or who are sitting partially outside of the school bus seats, will not be afforded the occupant protection provided by the school bus seats.

Small school buses must be equipped with lap and/or lap/shoulder belts at all designated seating positions. Since the sizes and weights of small school buses are closer to those of passenger cars and trucks, seat belts in those vehicles are necessary to provide occupant protection.

School Bus Drivers

Safe transportation of school children demands certified, trained and responsible drivers. The U.S. Department of Transportation requires school bus drivers to hold a Commercial Drivers License (CDL). The driver must also receive additional specialized training by the state. In addition, drivers must pass drug and alcohol screening tests and law enforcement background checks.

SHUTTLE BUS SERVICE

Shuttle bus service is a type of local bus service that provides transportation for passengers between specific destinations, e.g., airport to hotel service. In addition, universities often provide shuttle bus service between buildings for students, and small towns may provide shuttle bus service for senior citizens to and from supermarkets, shopping malls, etc.

CHARTER BUS SERVICE

Chartered bus services provide buses and drivers for hire. Thus if you need to arrange group travel to another state, e.g., for an event, a trip or on an on-going basis, you may want to hire a charter bus service.

As discussed below, options for charter bus travel include motorcoach, school bus, minibus and passenger van, depending on the number of people traveling. In addition, some states mandate that only school buses be used to transport school children.

Therefore, if your group is comprised of school children, you must check with your state authorities to find out whether there are any such requirements in your state. Some school bus operators are private companies under contract to the local school system, but provide transportation services with school buses to the general public for a fee.

There are a number of important issues to consider in making your hiring decision. For example, you should always check whether the bus is licensed and maintains the required level of insurance, as safety should be your primary consideration.

A list of consumer protection tips for charter bus transportation can be found in Appendix 12 of this Almanac.

Vehicle Type Selection

Number of Passengers

For large groups, a motorcoach is a good option. A motorcoach is generally used for long-distance travel. It typically contains reclining seats and does not provide any standing room. A motorcoach also contains a large space for storing luggage. A motorcoach transports approximately 40 to 50 passengers.

As discussed above, if you are required to use a school bus, they vary in size and seating capacity. Typically, a school bus can transport 10 to 80 passengers.

For smaller groups, a mini-bus has a smaller seating capacity than a motorcoach, and can typically transport about 16 or more passengers, and a passenger van generally transports 15 or fewer passengers.

It should be noted, however, that according to research conducted by the National Highway Traffic Safety Administration, 12 and 15-passenger vans have a rollover risk that rises significantly—to nearly three times the rollover rate—as the number of passengers increases from less than 5 to more than 10.

Length of Trip

An important factor in deciding which bus to use is the length of the trip. For safety reasons, drivers of vehicles used to transport 16 or more passengers in interstate commerce are subject to driving time limitations. Under Department of Transportation (DOT) regulations, a driver may not drive more than 10 hours following 8 consecutive hours off duty. In addition, drivers may not drive at all after 15 on-duty hours. Thus relief drivers may need to be hired to legally complete the trip.

Another consideration is comfort during a lengthy trip. In general, a motorcoach is more comfortable for passengers and drivers on a long trip. Many motorcoaches have restroom facilities that can be used while the vehicle is in operation. School buses, mini-buses and vans do not have such facilities. In addition, the type and style of seating on the vehicle should also be considered when planning a long trip.

Storage Consideration

If passengers will be bringing baggage or equipment on the trip, you must consider the availability of storage space. It is unsafe to keep baggage and equipment in the bus aisles or stacked in empty seats. Nearly all motorcoaches have storage areas for luggage and equipment. School buses generally have little or no storage capacity, and the storage capacity of mini-buses and vans is limited. It is important, therefore, to check with the company to determine whether there is enough storage space to meet your needs.

Tour Bus Service

Tour buses operate in popular tourist destinations. Generally, a tour guide provides passengers information with interesting and anecdotal information as the bus passes tourist sites on a predetermined route. In some cases, the bus may stop and allow passengers to spend time at sites of particular interest.

Executive Coach Service

Executive coaches are spacious buses that offer communications technology that affords companies the ability to conduct mobile press conferences, sales presentations and en route strategy sessions. Executive coaches may include a refreshment bar, DVD player, wet bar and wireless Internet capabilities.

GREYHOUND LINES

Founded in 1914, Greyhound Lines, Inc. is the largest provider of intercity bus transportation, serving more than 2,300 destinations with 13,000 daily departures across North America and more than 1,700 destinations in the United States.

Greyhound Lines serves approximately 25 million passengers each year. The top 10 busiest terminals are New York, NY; Philadelphia, PA; Atlantic City, NJ; Richmond, VA; Los Angeles, CA; Washington, DC; Atlanta, GA; Baltimore, MD; Nashville, TN; and Dallas, TX.

While Greyhound is well known for its regularly scheduled passenger service, the company also provides a number of other services for its customers. For example, Greyhound Travel Services offers charter packages for businesses, conventions, schools and other groups.

In addition, Greyhound has interline partnerships with a number of independent bus lines across the United States. These bus companies provide complementary service to Greyhound's existing schedules and link to many of the smaller towns in Greyhound's national route system.

Amtrak passengers use Greyhound to make connections to cities not served by rail on Amtrak Thruway service, by purchasing a ticket for the bus connection from Amtrak in conjunction with the purchase of their rail ticket. If passengers desire, they may also buy a bus ticket directly from Greyhound.

Travel within Canada

For travel within Canada, Greyhound Canada carries millions of passengers across Canada's provinces and territories each year.

Travel from Mexico

For those within Mexico who wish to travel by Greyhound in the United States, Greyhound subsidiary, Greyhound de Mexico, can sell Greyhound tickets at one of more than 100 agencies located throughout Mexico. The agencies also sell tickets for several Mexican bus companies, which connect to Greyhound service at the United States-Mexico border cities.

TRAILWAYS TRANSPORTATION SYSTEMS

Trailways Transportation System is a franchise organization comprised of independently-owned transportation companies as well as tour and travel-related service entities. Trailways was founded in 1936 and was originally known as the National Trailways Bus System.

The Trailways system consists of 80 transportation member companies located in 32 states, Ontario, Canada, Germany and The Netherlands. Trailways members provide charter bus and motorcoach rental service and tours, as well as scheduled routes and shuttle services.

A list of Trailways Transportation Member Companies and their locations can be found in Appendix 13 of this Almanac.

THE FEDERAL MOTOR CARRIER SAFETY REGULATIONS

As part of the U.S. Department of Transportation, the Federal Motor Carrier Safety Administration (FMCSA) is the agency responsible for bus safety. Its mission is to reduce highway fatalities while ensuring the safe interstate transportation of passengers.

The FMCSA issues, administers and enforces the Federal Motor Carrier Safety Regulations and Commercial Regulations that apply to commercial motor vehicles that transport passengers. FMCSA's Commercial Passenger Carrier Safety Division within the agency's headquarters develops policies, plans and guidance in matters related to commercial passenger safety. The FMCSA regulations are set forth in Title 49 of the Code of Federal Regulations (CFR).

Passenger Carrier Regulations

The Passenger Carrier Regulations enforced by the FMCSA are set forth at 49 CFR Part 374. Selected provisions are discussed below.

Discrimination Prohibited

Pursuant to 49 CFR § 374.101, et seq.: "No motor common carrier of passengers . . . shall operate a motor vehicle in interstate or foreign commerce on which the seating of passengers is based upon race, color, creed, or national origin."

The regulations also require that every ticket sold by a common carrier of passengers for transportation in interstate or foreign commerce contain a plainly legible notice that states: "Seating aboard vehicles operated in interstate or foreign commerce is without regard to race, color, creed, or national origin." The notice need only appear once on the ticket, even if the ticket consists of multiple parts, such as a stub or coupon. However, the notice must be placed on the face of the part of the ticket that is held by the passenger.

The regulations further require that the terminal facilities of such common carriers cannot be arranged or maintained so as to involve any separation or restriction in the use of the terminal facility on the basis of race, color, creed or national origin. A conspicuously displayed notice must be posted in the terminal facility and maintained so that it is readily visible to the public. The notice must contain the full text of the regulations. Terminal facilities subject to these regulations include waiting rooms, restrooms and any areas set aside for eating, drinking and ticket sales that are made available to passengers.

If any "person, municipality, county or parish, state or body politic" interferes with the requirements of the regulations, the carrier is required to make a report within 15 days of the occurrence, including a statement of the action that the carrier may have taken to eliminate the interference.

Smoking Ban

Pursuant to 49 CFR § 374.201, smoking is prohibited on all motor common carriers of passengers. The smoking ban includes the carrying of lit cigars, cigarettes and pipes. The carriers are required to take necessary action to ensure that the smoking ban is followed, including making announcements to passengers, posting the international no-smoking symbol and posting legible no-smoking signs in all vehicles transporting passengers.

Ticketing and Information

Pursuant to 49 CFR § 374.305, carrier terminal facilities and stations must provide information as to schedules, tickets, fares, baggage and other carrier services during business hours. Printed route schedules must be provided at all facilities where tickets are sold, and each schedule must show the points along the carrier's routes where facilities are located, and the arrival and departure time for each point.

In addition, the carrier's ticketing agents and personnel, who provide information concerning ticketing and carrier services, are required to be adequately informed.

Further, every facility where tickets are sold is required to provide a telephone information service to transmit information to the public, including current schedules and fare information.

Each carrier must refund unused tickets upon request, at each place where tickets are sold, within 30 days after the request.

All terminals and stations must provide adequate security and be regularly patrolled.

Baggage Rules

Pursuant to 49 CFR § 374.307, carriers must issue receipts for all checked services baggage. If the baggage checking service is not provided at the side of the carrier, all baggage checked at a baggage checking counter at least 30 minutes but not more than 1 hour before departure must be transported on the same schedule as the ticketed passenger.

If baggage checking service is provided at the side of the carrier, passengers checking baggage at the baggage checking counter less than 30 minutes before the scheduled departure shall be notified that their baggage may not travel on the same schedule. Such baggage must then be placed on the next available carrier to its destination. However, all baggage checked at the side of the carrier during boarding, or at alternative locations provided for such purpose, shall be transported on the same schedule as the ticketed passenger.

Passengers must securely attach their identification to each item of baggage checked, indicating in a clear and legible manner the name and address to which the baggage should be forwarded if lost and subsequently recovered. A carrier must make identification tags available to its passengers upon request. All checked baggage must be placed in a secure or attended area prohibited to the public. In addition, baggage being readied for loading must not be left unattended.

No carrier may totally exempt its liability for items offered as checked baggage, unless those items have been exempted by the Secretary of Transportation. A notice listing exempted items must be prominently posted at every location where baggage is accepted for checking.

Carriers may refuse to accept as checked baggage and, if unknowingly accepted, may disclaim liability for loss or damage to the following articles:

1. articles whose transportation as checked baggage is prohibited by law or regulation;

2. fragile or perishable articles, articles whose dimensions exceed the size limitations in the carrier's tariff, receptacles with articles attached or protruding, guns and materials which have a disagreeable odor;

3. money; and

4. those other articles that the Secretary of Transportation exempts upon petition by the carrier.

Lost Baggage

All checked baggage must be made available to the passenger within a reasonable time not to exceed 30 minutes after arrival at the passenger's destination. If not, the carrier shall deliver the baggage to the passenger's local address at the carrier's expense.

Checked baggage that cannot be located within one hour after the arrival of the carrier upon which it is supposed to be transported is designated as lost. The carrier must notify the passenger at that time and furnish the passenger with an appropriate tracing form. A single form for both tracing baggage and filing a claim must be made available at each ticket window and baggage counter.

The passenger and the carrier's representative must sign the tracing form, in duplicate. The carrier or its agent will retain the signed original, with any necessary documentation and additional information, and the claim check, for which a receipt shall be given. The passenger will be given the duplicate copy. The carrier is required to make immediate and diligent efforts to recover lost baggage.

In addition to checked baggage, a passenger may fill out a tracing form for lost unchecked baggage. The carrier is required to forward recovered unchecked baggage to the terminal or station nearest the address shown on the tracing form, and to notify the passenger that the baggage will be held on a will-call basis.

Lost checked baggage that cannot be located within 15 days is processed by the carrier as a claim. The date that the carrier receives the tracing form is considered the first day of a 60-day period in which a lost baggage claim must be resolved by a firm offer of settlement or by a written denial of the claim.

Excess Value Declaration–Permissible Limitations

Pursuant to 49 CFR § 374.401, common carriers of passengers and baggage may not publish tariff provisions limiting their liability for loss or damage to baggage checked by a passenger transported in regular route or special operations unless the amount for which liability is limited is $250 or greater per adult fare. The carriers may publish a maximum value for which they will be liable, but that maximum value may not be less than $1,000.

For an additional charge, passengers are permitted to declare a value in excess of the limited amount, and recover that increased amount in the event of loss or damage, provided that their recovery is not higher than the actual value of the luggage.

Further, carriers need not offer excess value coverage on articles of extraordinary value, including, but not limited to, negotiable instruments, papers, manuscripts, irreplaceable publications, documents, jewelry and watches.

Pursuant to 49 CFR § 374.403, a notice of the passenger's ability to declare excess value on their baggage must be provided to the public. The notice must be in large and clear print, and state as follows:

NOTICE—BAGGAGE LIABILITY

This motor carrier is not liable for loss or damage to properly identified baggage in an amount exceeding $_____. If a passenger desires additional coverage for the value of his baggage he may, upon checking his baggage, declare that his baggage has a value in excess of the above limitation and pay a charge as follows:

IDENTIFY YOUR BAGGAGE

Under FMCSA regulations, all baggage must be properly identified. Luggage tags should indicate clearly the name and address to which lost baggage should be forwarded. Free luggage tags are available at all ticket windows and baggage counters.

The notice must be placed at the following locations: (1) near the ticket seller; (2) near any location where baggage may be checked; and (3) at each boarding point or waiting area used by the carrier at facilities maintained by the carrier or its agents. The notice placed at these locations must be sufficiently conspicuous so as to alert each passenger of the provisions concerning the availability of excess value coverage. In addition, the notice must appear on a form to be attached to each ticket issued.

Security at Terminal Facilities

Pursuant to 49 CFR § 374.309, all terminals and stations must provide adequate security for passengers and their attendants, and must be regularly patrolled. At terminals and stations that are closed when buses are scheduled to arrive or depart, there shall be available, to the extent possible, a public telephone, outside lighting, posted schedule information, overhead shelter, information on local accommodations and telephone numbers for local taxi service and police.

Service Responsibilities

Pursuant to 49 CFR § 374.311, all carriers are responsible for providing passengers with information regarding transportation schedules and assist passengers with any scheduling problems.

Regarding scheduling, carriers are required to establish schedules that can be reasonably met, and must provide a sufficient number of buses to meet their passengers' normal travel demands, including increased demand during seasonal or holiday periods.

In addition, if there will be a change to an existing regular-route schedule, the carrier must first file a written notice with the FMCSA Division Office. A copy of the notice must also be conspicuously displayed in each facility and on each affected bus for a reasonable period of time before the effective date of the schedule change. The notice must set forth the availability of alternative service and contain carrier contact information for passengers. To the extent possible, the carrier must mitigate any inconvenience it causes by disrupting a passenger's travel plans.

Equipment

Pursuant to 49 CFR § 374.313, the carrier must keep the buses clean and maintain a reasonable temperature. In addition, every bus that seats more than 14 passengers must have a clean, regularly maintained restroom. However, if the bus makes reasonable rest stops, it may be operated without a restroom.

Transportation of Passengers with Disabilities

Pursuant to 49 CFR § 374.315, service provided by a carrier to passengers with disabilities is governed by the provisions of 42 U.S.C. § 12101, which states, in part:

42 U.S.C. § 12142. Public Entities Operating Fixed Route Systems

(a) Purchase and lease of new vehicles

It shall be considered discrimination...for a public entity which operates a fixed route system to purchase or lease a new bus...if such bus...is not readily accessible to and usable by individuals with disabilities, including individuals who use wheelchairs.

(b) Purchase and lease of used vehicles

It shall be considered discrimination...for a public entity which operates a fixed route system to purchase or lease . . . a used vehicle for use on such system unless such entity makes demonstrated good faith efforts to purchase or lease a used vehicle for use on such system that is readily accessible to and usable by individuals with disabilities, including individuals who use wheelchairs.

***

42 U.S.C. § 12148. Public Transportation Programs and Activities in Existing Facilities

(a) Public transportation programs and activities in existing facilities

(1) In general

With respect to existing facilities used in the provision of designated public transportation services, it shall be considered discrimination . . . for a public entity to fail to operate a designated public transportation program or activity conducted in such facilities so that, when viewed in the entirety, the program or activity is readily accessible to and usable by individuals with disabilities.

Identification Requirement

Pursuant to 49 CFR § 374.317, each bus and driver providing service must be identified in a manner visible to passengers. The driver may be identified by name or company number.

Qualifications of Drivers

The Qualifications of Drivers Regulations are set forth at 49 CFR Part 391. The purpose of these regulations is to establish minimum qualifications for persons who drive commercial motor vehicles and minimum duties of motor carriers with respect to the qualifications of their drivers.

Selected provisions are discussed below.

General Qualifications of Drivers

Pursuant to 49 CFR § 391.111, a person is qualified to driver a commercial motor vehicle if he or she:

1. is at least 21 years old;

2. can read and speak the English language sufficiently to converse with the general public, to understand highway traffic signs and signals in the English language, to respond to official inquiries, and to make entries on reports and records;

3. can, by reason of experience, training, or both, safely operate the type of commercial motor vehicle he or she drives;

4. is physically qualified to drive a commercial motor vehicle in accordance with the Physical Qualifications and Examinations of [this part];

5. has a currently valid commercial motor vehicle operator's license issued only by one State or jurisdiction;

6. has prepared and furnished the motor carrier that employs him or her with the list of violations or the certificate as required by this part;

7. is not disqualified to drive a commercial motor vehicle under the rules in [this part]; and

8. has successfully completed a driver's road test and has been issued a certificate of driver's road test in accordance with [this part], or has presented an operator's license or a certificate of road test which the motor carrier that employs him or her has accepted as equivalent to a road test in accordance with [this part].

Responsibilities of Drivers

Pursuant to 49 CFR § 391.113, a motor carrier shall not require or permit a person to drive a commercial motor vehicle unless the person:

(a) can, by reason of experience, training, or both, determine whether the cargo he/she transports—including baggage in a passenger-carrying commercial motor vehicle—has been properly located, distributed, and secured in or on the commercial motor vehicle he/she drives; and (b) is familiar with methods and procedures for securing cargo in or on the commercial motor vehicle he or she drives.

Controlled Substances and Alcohol Use and Testing Regulations

The Controlled Substances and Alcohol Use and Testing Regulations enforced by the FMCSA are set forth at 49 CFR Part 382. The purpose of these regulations is to establish programs designed to help prevent accidents and injuries resulting from the misuse of alcohol or use of controlled substances by drivers of commercial motor vehicles performing "safety-sensitive functions."

"Safety-sensitive function" means all time from the time a driver begins to work or is required to be in readiness to work until the time he or she is relieved from work and all responsibility for performing work.

Selected provisions are discussed below.

On-Duty Use

Pursuant to 49 CFR § 382.205, drivers are prohibited from using alcohol while performing "safety-sensitive" functions. If the employer has actual knowledge that the driver is using alcohol during this time, the employer may not permit the driver to perform or continue to perform such functions.

Pre-Duty Use

Pursuant to 49 CFR § 382.207, drivers are prohibited from performing safety-sensitive functions within four hours after using alcohol. If the employer has actual knowledge that the driver is using alcohol within four hours of using alcohol, the employer may not permit the driver to perform safety-sensitive functions.

Use Following an Accident

Pursuant to 49 CFR § 382.209, any driver required to take a post-accident alcohol test is not permitted to use alcohol for eight hours following the accident, or until he or she undergoes a post-accident alcohol test, whichever occurs first.

Controlled Substances Use

Pursuant to 49 CFR § 382.213, drivers are prohibited from using controlled substances while performing "safety-sensitive" functions, except when the use is pursuant to the instructions of a licensed medical practitioner who has advised the driver that the substance will not adversely affect the driver's ability to safely operate a commercial motor vehicle.

If the employer has actual knowledge that the driver is using a controlled substance, the employer may not permit the driver to perform or continue to perform a safety-sensitive function. In addition, the employer may require the driver to inform the employer of any therapeutic drug use.

Refusal to Submit to Alcohol or Controlled Substances Test

Pursuant to 49 CFR § 382.211, no driver shall refuse to submit to a post-accident alcohol or controlled substances test, a random alcohol or controlled substances test, a reasonable suspicion alcohol or controlled substances test, or a follow-up alcohol or controlled substances test. Further, the employer must not allow a driver who refuses to submit to such tests to perform or continue to perform safety-sensitive functions.

CHAPTER 6:
CRUISE SHIPS

IN GENERAL

A cruise ship is basically a large boat that is designed to carry passengers for pleasure trips to various ports around the world. The ship is equipped with numerous amenities that provide enjoyment and relaxation for millions of passengers each year. The ships generally leave and return to the same port.

In the 19th and early 20th centuries, cruising was a practice enjoyed by the wealthy, who opted to sail to warmer climates during the winter. At that time, large luxurious ocean liners were the vessel of choice, having previously been used primarily for transatlantic voyages.

In the mid-20th century, air travel became a more popular and expedient method of transportation. The ocean liner industry declined, giving way to smaller cruise ships. As cruising vacations became more affordable and gained popularity, larger ships were built to accommodate the growing number of passengers. Since 1980, the North American cruise industry, which makes up the majority of the global cruise market, has experienced an average annual passenger growth rate of 8.1%. Cruising is expected to continue to gain popularity, with an estimated 20.7 million cruise travelers in 2010.

Cruise capacity also increased by 450% over the same period. Cruise ships now carry upwards of 3,000 passengers on one trip, and the North American cruise industry has had overall passenger occupancies at full capacity in recent years. In 2005, 9.8 million people took North American cruise vacations, the majority of whom were U.S. residents.

Initially, cruise ships traveled close to home, e.g., to Mexico and the Caribbean. Now, passengers can travel to virtually every area of the world, with top destinations being the Caribbean, the Mediterranean,

Alaska, Europe and the west coast of Mexico. Cruise destinations are also expanding to include continents and areas not easily accessible by other means of travel.

A directory of international cruise lines and associated ships can be found in Appendix 14 of this Almanac.

REGISTRY REQUIREMENT

Cruise ships engaged in international commerce fly flags of registry, which are required for operation in international waters. Cruise lines often choose to register either in their country of ownership or ship production. Many cruise ships are registered in the United Kingdom, Liberia, Panama, Norway, the Netherlands, the Bahamas and the United States.

Flag registry countries are required to provide comprehensive maritime expertise, require annual safety inspections before issuance of a passenger vessel certificate and monitor vessel compliance with international maritime laws, as well as flag state standards.

Some cruise lines register in countries that have lenient maritime registration rules, because of their reduced safety and crew requirements. Their flags of registry are generally referred to as "Flags of Convenience."

JURISDICTION

Cruise ships are governed by maritime law. This can be confusing when trying to determine which law applies in a particular situation, as each country has its own maritime laws. As set forth above, each ship is required to obtain a registry flag from the country where it is registered, and the laws of that country generally apply to that ship, with some exceptions.

The law of the port country will apply when a ship is docked in the internal waters of the country, such as the ports and bays. Thus if a ship registered in Norway is docked in a New York port, the laws of the United States govern. In addition, the port country's laws also apply in territorial waters, which extend up to 12 miles from the country's shoreline.

Within the area between 12 and 24 miles from the shoreline—known as the contiguous zone—the port country maintains certain limited rights, such as the right to patrol its borders. However, when the ship travels beyond 24 miles from the port country's shoreline, it is in international waters, and the law of the country where the ship is registered governs. Thus when the Norwegian ship leaves New York, Norwegian law applies once the ship reaches international waters.

HEALTH ISSUES

In the United States, the U.S. Coast Guard enforces maritime safety requirements, and the Centers for Disease Control (CDC) has regulatory responsibilities for sanitation and public health on cruise ships bound for a U.S. port from a foreign port. As discussed below, a major medical concern aboard cruise ships is the spread of infectious diseases among passengers and crew.

Transmission of Illness on Cruise Ships

There have been a number of reports where hundreds of passengers aboard a single cruise ship have come down with the same illness. It has been found that the time spent on a cruise ship correlates with the spread of onboard illness. Gambling cruises may last for several hours, while passengers on world cruises can travel for months. The average duration of a pleasure cruise, however, is approximately 7 days.

Thus the longer time passengers spend on the ship, the more likely it is that they will be exposed to a communicable disease, e.g., through person-to-person contact, or contaminated food and water. Contamination of whirlpool spas and potable water supply systems have most commonly been implicated as sources of infection.

These large ships carry passengers from all areas of the world, who often have diverse medical and immunization backgrounds and health risk behaviors. In fact, clusters of rubella and varicella have been investigated on cruises originating in the U.S., highlighting the potential of global dissemination of vaccine-preventable diseases through cruise travel.

In addition, as passengers disembark at various ports, they risk contracting disease exposure that they then bring back on board and spread throughout the ship, as well as the communities to which they return. Thus detecting and preventing infectious diseases acquired during cruises are important not only to protect the health of cruise travelers but also to avoid a global dissemination of diseases.

Heightened disease surveillance efforts by cruise lines in cooperation with public health authorities and awareness among cruise ship travelers have led to the detection of illnesses of potential public health significance that might otherwise have gone unnoticed.

Age Factor

Although communicable diseases occurring onboard cruise ships reflect similar onshore events, transmission risk is enhanced due to close contact among the passengers. Senior citizens are particularly vulnerable due to underlying chronic health problems and a compromised immune system.

If an older passenger contracts an illness, recovery may take longer, and he or she is at increased risk of morbidity. A study of cruise ship medical logs showed that over one-half of infirmary visits are made by passengers over the age of 65. The most common diagnosis is respiratory tract infection, followed by injuries, seasickness and GI illness.

Outbreaks

In recent years, onboard outbreaks of viral gastroenteritis and Legionnaires' disease have been particularly problematic.

Viral Gastroenteritis

Gastroenteritis refers to inflammation of the stomach and small and large intestines. Viral gastroenteritis is an infection caused by a variety of viruses that result in vomiting, diarrhea, headache, fever and abdominal cramps. It is often called the "stomach flu," although it is not caused by an influenza virus.

Viral gastroenteritis is not caused by bacteria, such as *Salmonella* or *E. Coli*, or by parasites, such as *Giardia*, or by medications or other medical conditions, although the symptoms may be similar. Viral gastroenteritis is caused by a virus. Noroviruses are a group of viruses that cause viral gastroenteritis.

In general, the symptoms begin 1 to 2 days following exposure to a virus that causes gastroenteritis and may last for 1 to 10 days, depending on which virus causes the illness. For most people, viral gastroenteritis is not serious, and they recovery completely without any long-term problems. However, persons who are unable to drink enough fluids, such as infants, young children, disabled or elderly, are at risk of dehydration, and this may lead to hospitalization.

Unfortunately for cruise ships passengers, viral gastroenteritis is contagious. The illness is spread through close contact with infected persons, e.g., by sharing food, water, or eating utensils. Individuals may also become infected by eating or drinking contaminated foods or beverages.

Legionnaires' Disease

Unlike viral gastroenteritis, Legionnaires' disease is caused by bacteria known as *legionella*. Legionella has been known to infect the water supply system. The bacteria got its name in 1976, when many people who went to a Philadelphia convention of the American Legion suffered from an outbreak of this disease. Each year, between 8,000 and 18,000 people are hospitalized with the illness in the United States.

Legionnaires' disease is a type of pneumonia, and can have symptoms like many other forms of pneumonia. Signs of the disease can include a high fever, chills and a cough. Some people may also suffer from muscle aches and headaches. These symptoms usually begin 2 to 14 days after being exposed to the bacteria.

Legionnaires' disease can be very serious and can cause death in up to 5% to 30% of cases. However, most people can be treated successfully with antibiotics, and healthy people usually recover from infection. People at high risk include the elderly, smokers and those with chronic lung disease or a weakened immune system.

People get Legionnaires' disease when they breathe in a mist or vapor that has been contaminated with the bacteria. The bacteria are not spread from one person to another person. Outbreaks have been linked with cruise ships, with the most likely sources being whirlpool spas, and water used for drinking and bathing.

Illness Prevention

According to the CDC, if you intend to take a cruise, you should follow these tips to try and prevent contracting a communicable illness onboard the ship.

You should wash your hands before touching your hand to your mouth, including eating and drinking, smoking, brushing your teeth and helping a sick person.

You should wash your hands after using the bathroom; changing diapers; touching hand contact surfaces, such as door knobs and railings; returning to your cabin; helping a sick person; and blowing your nose.

In order to properly wash your hands, you should wet your hands with warm water, apply a generous amount of soap, rub your hands together for 20 seconds; rinse your hands, and dry your hands with a paper towel; and use a paper towel to turn off the faucet and open the exit door.

The CDC recommends that cruise ship passengers use warm water and soap to wash their hands; however, if water and soap are not available, you should use an ethanol alcohol-based hand sanitizer.

You should leave the area if you see someone getting sick, e.g., coughing, vomiting, etc. You risk becoming sick if you inhale contaminated particles that travel through the air. In addition, you should report the incident to the cruise staff.

You should take care of yourself by getting plenty of rest, which helps rebuild your immune system. In addition, you should drink a lot of water to prevent dehydration.

Prevention Medications and Immunizations

Due to multiple port visits and potential exposures, cruise ship passengers must find out whether there are any prevention medications or immunizations that they need considering their destinations. Prior to traveling, you should ask your health care provider for destination-specific recommended and required vaccines, as well as prevention medication, if needed.

You should also make sure you are up-to-date on your vaccinations. If motion sickness is a problem, you should request an appropriate medication. In addition, in case you require onboard medical treatment, you should bring a written summary of your medical history with you on the ship.

Cruise Ship Medical Facilities

According to the ACEP Health Care Guidelines on Cruise Ship Medical Facilities, published by the Cruise Ship and Maritime Medicine Section of the American College of Emergency Physicians (ACEP) in 2000, large cruise lines that operate in the United States must meet or exceed the ACEP guideline standards.

The guidelines for the cruise ship's medical facility include provisions for: (1) an isolation room to manage communicable diseases; (2) diagnostic and emergency medical equipment; (3) a formulary; (4) staff number and qualifications; and (5) a health, hygiene and safety program for medical personnel.

An estimated 95% of illnesses seen in cruise ship medical facilities can be treated onboard. In addition, injuries are one of the most common reasons for passengers to seek medical care on cruise ships, accounting for about 18% of passenger infirmary visits. However, a passenger with a serious injury or medical problem must be transferred to an on-shore hospital after he or she is stabilized.

Nevertheless, cruise ship passengers should be aware that the ACEP guidelines for large cruise lines may not be followed by smaller ships or those run by independent operators. In fact, there may be no medical provisions onboard such ships.

In addition, there are no uniform, international standards for medical care aboard a cruise ship, and you may be treated by a medical provider who is not trained or licensed to practice medicine in the United States.

Cruise ship passengers with chronic diseases or those who may require comprehensive medical care during travel should consult with their health care providers and notify the cruise line of special needs before travel, such as wheelchair access, oxygen tank, dialysis, etc. In addition, special cruises are now available for passengers who have certain medical conditions.

Vessel Sanitation Program

In 1975, in response to several large gastrointestinal disease outbreaks on cruise ships, the CDC established the Vessel Sanitation Program (VSP), a joint cooperative program with the cruise industry. The goal of the program is to minimize the risk of gastrointestinal disease on cruise ships.

The VSP encourages the cruise industry to establish and maintain a comprehensive sanitation program, including surveillance for acute gastroenteritis. The staff conducts biannual, unannounced sanitation inspections on U.S.–bound cruise ships with international itineraries carrying 13 or more passengers.

The VSP also engages in the design and construction of new ships, as well as retrofitting older ones to enhance facilities and provisions that promote shipboard sanitation and public health. The VSP sanitation inspections cover the following areas of public health interest:

1. water supply storage, distribution, disinfection and protection;

2. spas and pools disinfection and filtration;

3. food handling, including storage, preparation and service;

4. the potential for contamination of food, water and ice;

5. personal hygiene and sanitation practices of crew;

6. general cleanliness and condition of the ship; and

7. ship training programs in environmental and public health practices.

An inspection score of 86 or higher out of 100 indicates an acceptable level of sanitation. In general, the higher the score, the higher the level of sanitation, but this score does not reflect the risk of acquiring gastrointestinal disease. If VSP inspectors find that sanitation deficiencies on a cruise ship could pose a public health threat, the VSP could recommend or require that a cruise ship not sail.

Recent sanitation scores and reports for specific cruise ships are posted on the CDC Website (http://www.cdc.gov/nceh/vsp/).

PASSENGERS WITH DISABILITIES

The cruise industry is primarily concerned with the safety and comfort of all passengers, including passengers with disabilities. The International Maritime Organization (IMO) is responsible for establishing international standards for cruise ship safety, design and construction. The IMO prepared passenger vessel guidelines that address design and operation features for accommodation of persons with disabilities.

The United States Department of Transportation (DOT) has not yet implemented regulations for accessibility standards on U.S. flag commercial vessels. The DOT has indicated that prior to promulgating a rule for commercial vessels, it must assess any potential conflicts with international design, construction and operation standards for ocean-going vessels.

In addition, the Passenger Vessel Access Advisory Committee (PVAAC) was established by the United States Architectural and Transportation Barriers Compliance Board. The objective of the committee is to provide recommendations regarding accessibility onboard and onto passenger cruise ships.

Although at this time there are no mandatory requirements governing passenger vessels, the cruise industry is dedicated to accommodating and improving accessibility for persons with disabilities on passenger cruise ships.

CRUISE SHIP GAMBLING

Gambling is provided on cruise ships for the enjoyment of cruise passengers. The minimum age for gambling on a cruise ship is usually 18 or 21, however, cruise ships are allowed to set their own minimum age for gambling, as well as drinking.

In general, cruise ships are not restricted by the laws of their port country. For example, in the United States, the minimum age for casino gambling is 21. However, once the cruise ship enters international waters, it is not subject to this restriction. Once the ship reaches a destination port, the rules of the port country apply.

The rules of play for gambling on cruise ships generally follow those established for casinos in Nevada, New Jersey or England. Each cruise line is required to provide a gaming guide setting forth the rules of play for their casino. The house rules must also be made available in every casino. In addition, each cruise line must post the minimum and maximum betting limits for each game at every gaming table.

All casinos are required to maintain detailed internal control measurers concerning the cash and coin counts, casino cage procedures and other procedures, similar to licensed jurisdictions. Each cruise line must employ some form of surveillance to assure operations are fair and equitable for all parties.

If there is a gaming dispute that cannot be resolved onboard the ship, a passenger may request contact information for the ship's home office, where the dispute can be pursued following the cruise.

CRUISE SHIP LIABILITY

In general, a cruise ship is responsible for the safe transportation of its passengers, and must comply with the safety regulations of the country in which the ship is registered. Thus if you are injured or a victim of a crime while traveling on a cruise ship, you are generally permitted to file a lawsuit and recover money for any damages you suffered, such as lost wages, medical bills and pain and suffering.

In addition to recovering for injuries you sustained onboard the ship, you may also recover for any injuries that occur ashore while the ship is docked in a port. You may be able to recover damages for your injuries from the tour operator if they were negligent in some way, e.g., they failed to advise passengers to stay away from a known crime area, or they hired an irresponsible local tour guide service to escort the passengers and injuries resulted.

The Cruise Ticket

You should familiarize yourself with your cruise ticket as your rights as a passenger and the liability of the cruise line are generally contained in your ticket. The cruise ticket is also referred to as a "contract of carriage."

Unfortunately, cruise ticket language and printing are not subject to any particular regulations, and may be difficult or impossible to read.

The font size may be so small as to be unreadable, and any attempt by a state to require a particular letter size is preempted by maritime law.

Many cruise lines will try to disclaim liability, and the waiver of liability will be set forth on the ticket. However, as common carriers, cruise ships are held to a very high standard of care for passengers, and a disclaimer of liability, particularly if injuries are caused by gross negligence or the intentional misconduct, may not be enforceable.

Nevertheless, the ticket is a contract between you and the cruise line, and the terms and conditions contained in the ticket are enforceable. Therefore, you should make sure your travel agent or the tour operator explains any provisions contained in the ticket that are unclear before you travel.

Forum Selection

In order to file a lawsuit, you must first determine where the lawsuit must be filed, and the law that applies. As set forth above, your ticket will contain a forum selection clause, and you must comply with the choice of jurisdiction that is set forth on the ticket. If you try to file your lawsuit in any other court, it will likely be dismissed.

Jurisdiction is important because it would be difficult and costly to travel to and from a foreign country to prosecute a personal injury claim. This is exactly why a cruise ship will place a forum selection clause in the ticket. They are expecting that most people will not pursue filing a lawsuit in a foreign jurisdiction.

In general, the law of the country of registry will govern accidents or crimes that occur onboard the ship. Additionally, for cruises ships that depart from a U.S. port, the law of the state where the ship was docked, as well as federal law, may govern.

Choice of Law

Your ticket will also set forth the choice of law that will apply to your case. Thus even if your case is heard in the United States, the law that applies may be from another country, e.g., Greece or China. In determining whether a choice of law clause is enforceable, the Court will take into consideration: (1) the law of the country where the ship's flag is registered; (2) the place where the injury occurred; (3) the place where the contract was entered into; (4) the law of the selected forum; and (5) whether enforcing the choice of law provision would be unjust.

The law applied to the case is important because it directly impacts the damages a passenger can recover. Many foreign jurisdictions drastically limit the amount of money an injured person can recover for pain and suffering and other damages.

Statute of Limitations

Under maritime law, there is generally a shortened statute of limitations that applies to injuries that occur on cruise ships using U.S. ports, usually one-year. This means that your lawsuit must be filed much sooner than a lawsuit must be filed under many state laws.

If you are corresponding with the cruise line to try and resolve a claim, you must always take into account the applicable statute of limitations. The cruise line is fully aware that the clock is ticking, and may continue to correspond with you regarding your claim, hoping that you will miss the deadline to file your lawsuit. If that occurs, your next letter from the cruise line will likely be a notice advising you that your claim is time-barred, and that they can no longer be sued. That will be the end of your claim.

In addition, your ticket may contain additional provisions that must be followed in order to file a lawsuit. For example, you may be required to file a notice of your claim to the cruise line as a prerequisite to filing a lawsuit.

APPENDIX 1:
AIRLINE PASSENGERS DENIED
BOARDING (JANUARY–JUNE 2008)

RANK	AIRLINE	VOLUNTARY	INVOLUNTARY
1	JETBLUE AIRWAYS	26	14
2	HAWAIIAN AIRLINES	198	36
3	AIRTRAN AIRWAYS	16,102	341
4	ALASKA AIRLINES	4,480	480
5	AMERICAN AIRLINES	35,546	3,371
6	NORTHWEST AIRLINES	29,084	1,963
7	FRONTIER AIRLINES	2,262	483
8	UNITED AIRLINES	42,707	2,774
9	SOUTHWEST AIRLINES	43,009	6,519
10	MESA AIRLINES	11,578	606
11	CONTINENTAL AIRLINES	20, 702	3,006
12	SKYWEST AIRLINES	13,039	861
13	DELTA AIRLINES	30,267	5,206
14	US AIRWAYS	47,520	4,602
15	AMERICAN EAGLE AIRLINES	690	318
16	PINNACLE AIRLINES	455	121
17	COMAIR	4,482	728
18	ATLANTIC SOUTHEAST AIRLINES	7,821	1,293
	TOTAL	310,328	32,332

Source: U.S. Department of Transportation, Office of Aviation Enforcement.

APPENDIX 2:
AIRLINE FLIGHT DELAYS (JUNE 2008)

AIRLINE	NUMBER OF SCHEDULED FLIGHTS	NUMBER OF SCHEDULED FLIGHTS ARRIVING LATE 70% OF THE TIME OR MORE	PERCENTAGE
AirTran Airways	781	23	2.9
Alaska Airlines	457	1	0.2
American Airlines	1721	220	12.8
American Eagle Airlines	1510	69	4.6
Atlantic Southeast Airlines	847	8	0.9
Comair	624	65	10.4
Continental Airlines	927	79	8.5
Delta Airlines	1328	29	2.2
ExpressJet Airlines	1209	118	9.8
Frontier Airlines	287	4	1.4
Hawaiian Airlines	176	0	0.0
JetBlue Airways	560	50	8.9
Mesa Airlines	754	62	8.2
Northwest Airlines	1087	45	4.1
Pinnacle Airlines	723	0	0.0

AIRLINE	NUMBER OF SCHEDULED FLIGHTS	NUMBER OF SCHEDULED FLIGHTS ARRIVING LATE 70% OF THE TIME OR MORE	PERCENTAGE
SkyWest Airlines	1714	32	1.9
Southwest Airlines	3465	38	1.1
United Airlines	1351	108	8.0
US Airways	1335	15	1.0
TOTAL	20,856	965	4.6

Source: U.S. Department of Transportation, Office of Aviation Enforcement.

APPENDIX 3:
MISHANDLED BAGGAGE COMPLAINTS
(JANUARY–JUNE 2008)

RANK	AIRLINE	TOTAL BAGGAGE REPORTS	PERCENTAGE PER 1,000 PASSSENGERS
1	HAWAIIAN AIRLINES	12,342	3.14%
2	AIRTRAN AIRWAYS	21,244	3.24%
3	JETBLUE AIRWAYS	36,795	3.38%
4	NORTHWEST AIRLINES	84,995	4.07%
5	CONTINENTAL AIRLINES	83,871	4.47%
6	ALASKA AIRLINES	269,340	5.03%
7	SOUTHWEST AIRLINES	269,340	5.03%
8	UNITED AIRLINES	148,005	5.36%
9	US AIRWAYS	144,176	5.62%
10	FRONTIER AIRLINES	28,883	5.63%
11	DELTA AIRLINES	184,896	6.05%
12	AMERICAN AIRLINES	253,277	6.67%
13	EXPRESSJET AIRLINES	56,597	7.26%
14	COMAIR	35,523	8.18%
15	SKYWEST AIRLINES	93,477	8.80%

RANK	AIRLINE	TOTAL BAGGAGE REPORTS	PERCENTAGE PER 1,000 PASSSENGERS
16	PINNACLE AIRLINES	45,258	8.92%
17	MESA AIRLINES	51,981	8.93%
18	ATLANTIC SOUTHEAST AIRLINES	62,638	10.07%
19	AMERIAN EAGLE AIRLINES	94,792	11.39%
	TOTAL	1,766,444	5.82

Source: U.S. Department of Transportation, Office of Aviation Enforcement.

APPENDIX 4:
DIRECTORY OF AIRLINE CUSTOMER RELATIONS DEPARTMENTS

AIRLINE	ADDRESS	TELEPHONE	WEBSITE
AirTran Airways	9955 AirTran Boulevard Orlando, Florida 32827	800-965-2107	www.airtran.com
Alaska Airlines	P.O. Box 24948 Seattle, Washington 98124	800-654-5669	www.alaskaair.com
Aloha Airlines	P.O. Box 30028 Honolulu, Hawaii 96820	888-771-2855	www.alohaairlines.com
American Airlines	P.O. Bo 619612 M/D 2400 DFW Airport, Texas 72561-9612	817-967-2000	www. aa.com/customerrelations
American Eagle Airlines	P.O. Bo 619612 M/D 2400 DFW Airport, Texas 72561-9612	817-967-2000	www. aa.com/customerrelations
Atlantic Southeast Airlines	100 Hartsfield Centre Parkway Suite 800 Atlanta, Georgia 30354	404-766-1400	www.flyasa.com
Comair	77 Comair Boulevard Erlanger, Kentucky 41018	800-964-2550	www.comair.com
Continental Airlines	P.O. Box 4607, NHCCR Houston, Texas 77210-4607	800-932-2732	www.continental.com
Delta Airlines	P.O. Box 20980 Atlanta, Georgia 30320-2980	404-715-1402	www.delta.com
ExpressJet Airlines	700 N. Sam Houston Parkway Suite 200 Houston, Texas 77067	832-353-1025	www.expressjet.com
Frontier Airlines	7001 Tower Road Denver, Colorado 80249-7312	720-374-4639	www.frontierairlines.com
Hawaiian Airlines	P.O. Box 30008 Honolulu, Hawaii 96820	888-246-8526	www.hawaiianair.com

AIRLINE	ADDRESS	TELEPHONE	WEBSITE
JetBlue Airways	P.O. Box 17435-7435 Salt Lake City, Utah 84117	801-365-2533	www.jetblue.com
Mesa Airlines	410 N. 44th Street, Suite 799 Phoenix, Arizona 85201	602-685-4000	www.mesa-air.com
Northwest Airlines	P.O. Box 1908 Minot, North Dakota 58702	701-420-6282	www.nwa.com/talk
Pinnacle Airlines	1689 Nonconnah Boulevard Suite 111 Memphis, Tennessee 38103	901-348-4282	www.nwairlink.com
SkyWest Airlines	444 South River Road St. George, Utah 84790	435-634-3400	www.skywest.com
Southwest Airlines	P.O. Box 36647 Dallas, Texas 75235-1647	214-792-4223	www.southwest.com
United Airlines	P.O. Box 66100 Chicago, Illinois 60666	877-228-1327	www.ual.com
US Airways	4000 E. Sky Harbor Boulevard Phoenix, Arizona 85034	866-523-5333	www.usairways.com

Source: Aviation Consumer Protection Division, Department of Transportation.

APPENDIX 5:
AIRLINE COMPLAINT CATEGORIES
(JANUARY–JUNE 2008)

RANK	COMPLAINT CATEGORY	NUMBER OF COMPLAINTS	SUB-CATEGORY
1	FLIGHT PROBLEMS Cancellations Delays Misconnections	1861	 809 545 300
2	BAGGAGE	1,237	
3	RESERVATIONS/TICKETING/ BOARDING	735	
4	CUSTOMER SERVICE	731	
5	REFUNDS	467	
6	OVERSALES	282	
7	DISABILITY	226	
8	FARES	201	
9	OTHER Frequent Flyer	 182	 139
10	DISCRIMINATION	55	
11	ADVERTISING	22	
12	ANIMALS	2	
	COMPLAINT TOTAL	6,001	

Source: U.S. Department of Transportation, Office of Aviation Enforcement.

APPENDIX 6:
AIR TRAVEL COMPLAINT FORM

Organization & Functions | Air Travel Problems/Complaints | Air Travel Consumer Report | Rules & Guidelines
Travel Tips & Publications | Airline Customer Service Plans | Service Cessations | Safety/Security Information

Air Travel Complaint/Comment Form

Personal Information:		
Your Name: Title: [▲▼] First Name: [ ] * Last Name: [ ] *		
I am [Passenger ▲▼]*		

Contact Information:		
Address: [ ]		
City: [ ]	State: [▲▼]	
Zip Code: [ ]	Home Phone: [ ]	
E-mail Address: [ ] *	Daytime Phone: [ ] *	
(Either E-mail Address or Daytime Phone is required)		

Complaint/Comment Information:

Airline/Company: [   ] * (If not listed select "OTHER")

Flight Date: [   ] (Date Format: mm/dd/yyyy)

Flight Itinerary: [   ] (Cities / Flight Number)

Description of Problem/Inquiry*:

Attach a File (Optional) :

File Name: (Choose File) no file selected

Please click the "Browse" button to select the file you wish to upload.

Items marked with a * are required.

If you use the web complaint form above, we would welcome any comments that you may have about that process.

APPENDIX 7:
CONSUMER COMPLAINTS, BY AIRLINE
(JANUARY–JUNE 2008)

RANK	AIRLINE	NUMBER OF COMPLAINTS	COMPLAINTS PER 100,000 ENPLANEMENTS
1	SOUTHWEST AIRLINES	159	0.30
2	EXPRESSJET AIRLINES	39	0.45
3	ALASKA AIRLINES	48	0.56
4	SKYWEST AIRLINES	62	0.59
5	JETBLUE AIRWAYS	75	0.67
6	HAWAIIAN AIRLINES	29	0.75
7	ATLANTIC SOUTHEAST AIRLINES	56	0.88
8	MESA AIRLINES	55	0.98
9	NORTHWEST AIRLINES	252	0.98
10	AIRTRAN AIRWAYS	122	1.00
11	FRONTIER AIRLINES	55	1.04
12	CONTINENTAL AIRLINES	273	1.12
13	AMERICAN EAGLE AIRLINES	99	1.17
14	COMAIR	52	1.18
15	PINNACLE AIRLINES	69	1.33

RANK	AIRLINE	NUMBER OF COMPLAINTS	COMPLAINTS PER 100,000 ENPLANEMENTS
16	AMERICAN AIRLINES	739	1.56
17	DELTA AIRLINES	691	1.95
18	US AIRWAYS	579	2.07
19	UNITED AIRLINES	677	2.10
	TOTAL COMPLAINTS	4,131	1.23

Source: U.S. Department of Transportation, Office of Aviation Enforcement.

APPENDIX 8:
AMTRAK LOST TICKET REFUND APPLICATION

AMTRAK

Lost Ticket Refund Application
Limitation of Liability and Indemnity Agreement

Last Name *(type or print legibly)*	First Name	Phone Number: — —

Street Address

City	State/Province	ZIP/Postal Code	*Be sure to make a copy of this application for your records before sending it.*

No claims will be processed until the lost ticket numbers are identified and a completed, signed application is received by Amtrak Customer Refunds, Box 70, 30th St., Station, 2955 Market Street, Philadelphia, PA 19104-2898.
- If you purchased the tickets directly from Amtrak, an Amtrak agent may be able to assist you with determining the ticket numbers.
- If you purchased the tickets from a travel agency, contact that agency for assistance in determining the ticket number.
- If you paid by credit card, the ticket numbers may appear on your credit card statement; if you paid by check, the ticket numbers may appear on your cancelled check.

Lost Ticket Numbers: —

Location where the lost tickets were purchased. _____ Date of Purchase: ___/___/___
How were the lost tickets paid for? ☐ Cash ☐ Check ☐ American Express ☐ Discover Card ☐ Diners Club
☐ Master Card ☐ Visa ☐ Air Travel Card ☐ Other *(describe)* _____
Tickets are missing because they were:
☐ Lost ☐ Stolen ☐ Destroyed ☐ Lifted in error by Amtrak on Train No. _____ on date ___/___/___

Were new tickets purchased? ☐Yes ☐ No
If yes, **attach the original receipts from the repurchased tickets to this application if**:
- The original tickets were not refundable, and you want a refund of the repurchase, rather than an exchange voucher.
- The original tickets were not refundable and not exchangeable, and you want any kind of adjustment (refund or exchange voucher).
- You want the refund to be based on the form of payment of the repurchased tickets rather than the form of payment of the original tickets.

How would you like Amtrak to refund your tickets? (check one)
☐ With the form of payment used to purchase the lost tickets; $75.00 service charge and 10% refund fee apply
☐ With the form of payment used to purchase the new tickets (if applicable); $75.00 service charge and 10% refund fee apply
☐ With a non-refundable exchange voucher good toward future Amtrak travel within one year; only a $75.00 service charge applies

Conditions of Refund:
1. The undersigned applicant hereby represents that the information on this Application is true and correct and that the tickets are owned by the applicant and have not been used by him or her, and that they have been lost, stolen, or destroyed.
2. The application must be submitted no later than one year after the purchase date of the lost tickets.
3. The ticket numbers of all lost tickets must be identified and all must have been paid for by the person whose name is at the top of this application.
4. The application will be processed five months after it has been received by Amtrak Customer Refunds.
5. No refund will be made if the lost tickets have been honored previously for transportation or refunded to or exchanged by any person.
6. A service charge of $75.00 will be imposed for processing this Application and claim, and will be deducted from the amount of the refund or exchange voucher.

AMTRAK LOST TICKET REFUND APPLICATION

7. A separate refund fee of 10% of the remaining amount that is actually refunded will also be imposed on all cash, check and credit refunds. To avoid this 10% refund fee, the applicant may elect to receive a non-refundable exchange voucher instead of a refund; the exchange voucher is not refundable but may be applied toward future Amtrak travel within one year of its issue.

8. If the original ticket is not refundable, an exchange voucher is the only option unless the original receipts from the repurchased tickets are attached to this application. In this case the form of the refund will be based on the form of payment of the repurchased tickets. If the original ticket is both not refundable and not exchangeable, no adjustment of any kind will be made unless new tickets were purchased and the original receipts are attached to this application.

9. If the lost ticket is found, the applicant must send the ticket, and a statement that a Lost Ticket Refund Application had been submitted, to Amtrak Customer Refunds.

10. All refunds are subject to audit.

11. **The applicant acknowledges that Amtrak will not be liable for failure to identify the person using a ticket, or presenting a ticket for refund, as being the true owner of the ticket. The applicant agrees to indemnify and hold Amtrak harmless against any and all loss, damage, claim, or expense, including, without limitation, reasonable attorney's fees which Amtrak may suffer or incur by reason for issuing such refund and/or the subsequent presentation of said ticket for transportation, refund or any other use whatsoever.**

Signature of Applicant: _____ Date: _____

Amtrak Use Only

☐ Refund Approved   Processed by _____ on date_____

Amount of lost tickets $ _____ less $75.00, less 10% refund fee $ _____ Net refund $ _____☐ Check ☐ credit card
OR less service charge $75.00 Exchange voucher amount $ _____   Voucher No. _____

☐ Refund Denied   Reason: ☐ Ticket used on Train No. _____ on date _____

            ☐ Ticket Previously Refunded   ☐ Ticket Exchanged at _____ on date _____

            ☐ Other _____

NRPC 3237   Amtrak is a registered service mark of the National Railroad Passenger Corporation.

APPENDIX 9:
DIRECTORY OF RAPID TRANSIT SYSTEMS IN THE UNITED STATES

CITY	STATE	RAPID TRANSIT SYSTEM	WEBSITE
Atlanta	Georgia	Metropolitan Atlanta Rapid Transit Authority (MARTA)	www.itsmarta.com/
Baltimore	Maryland	Metro Subway (Baltimore Metro)	www.mtamaryland.com/
Boston	Massachusetts	Massachusetts Bay Transportation Authority (MBTA)	www.mbta.com/
Buffalo	New York	Buffalo Metro Rail	www.nfta.com/metro/
Chicago	Illinois	Chicago L	www.chicago-l.org/
Cleveland	Ohio	RTA Rapid Transit (The Rapid)	www.gcrta.org/
Los Angeles	California	Los Angeles County Metro Rail	www.metro.net/
Miami	Florida	Miami-Dade Metrorail	www.miamidade.gov/transit/
New York	New York	New York City Subway Metropolitan Transportation Authority (MTA)	www.mta.info/

CITY	STATE	RAPID TRANSIT SYSTEM	WEBSITE
New York	New York	Port Authority Trans-Hudson (PATH)	www.panynj.gov/CommutingTravel/path/html/
Philadelphia	Pennsylvania	Southeastern Pennsylvania Transportation Authority (SEPTA)	www.septa.com/
Philadelphia	Pennsylvania	Port Authority Transit Corporation (PATCO)	www.ridepatco.org/
Pittsburgh	Pennsylvania	Port Authority of Allegheny County (The T)	www.portauthority.org/paac/
St. Louis	Missouri	Metrolink	www.metrostlouis.org/
San Francisco Bay Area	California	The San Francisco Bay Area Rapid Transit District (BART)	www.bart.gov/
Washington, D.C.		Metrorail	www.wmata.com/

Source: NationMaster Online Encylopedia.

APPENDIX 10:
DIRECTORY OF COMMUTER RAIL SYSTEMS IN THE UNITED STATES

CITY	STATE	RAIL SYSTEM	WEBSITE
Albuquerque	New Mexico	RailRunner (New Mexico Rail Runner)	www.nmrailrunner.com/
Alexandria	Virginia	Virginia Railway Express (VRE)	www.vre.org/
Anchorage	Alaska	Alaska Railroad Corporation (ARC)	www.akrr.com/
Baltimore	Maryland	Maryland Transit Administration, MTA (MARC)	www.mtamaryland.com/
Boston	Massachusetts	Massachusetts Bay Transportation Authority (MBTA)	www.mbta.com/
Chesterton	Indiana	Northern Indiana Commuter Transportation District (NICTD)	www.nictd.com/
Chicago	Illinois	Northeast Illinois Regional Commuter Railroad Corporation (METRA)	www.metrarail.com/

CITY	STATE	RAIL SYSTEM	WEBSITE
Dallas	Texas	Trinity Railway Express (TRE)	www.trinityrailwayexpress.org/
Los Angeles	California	Southern California Regional Rail Authority (Metrolink)	www.metrolinktrains.com/
Nashville	Tennessee	Regional Transportation Authority, RTA (Music City Star)	http://rtarelaxandride.com/services/rail/index.html
New Haven	Connecticut	Connecticut Department of Transportation Shore Line East (SLE)	www.shorelineeast.com/
New York Long Island	New York	Long Island Rail Road (LIRR)	www.lirr.org/lirr/index.html
New York (northern suburbs and Connecticut)	New York/ Connecticut	Metro-North Railroad (MNRR)	www.mnr.org/mnr/
Newark	New Jersey	New Jersey Transit Corporation (NJT)	www.njtransit.com/
Oceanside	California	North County Transit District, NCTD (Coaster)	www.gonctd.com/
Philadelphia	Pennsylvania	Southeastern Pennsylvania Transit Authority (SEPTA)	www.septa.org/
Pompano Beach	Florida	South Florida Regional Transportation Authority (Tri-Rail)	www.tri-rail.com/
San Carlos	California	Peninsula Corridor Joint Powers Board (CALTRAIN)	www.caltrain.com/
Seattle	Washington	Central Puget Sound Regional Transportation Authority (Sound Transit)	www.soundtransit.org/
Stockton	California	Altamont Commuter Express (ACE)	www.acerail.com/

Source: American Public Transportation Association.

APPENDIX 11:
AMERICAN BUS ASSOCIATION
CODE OF ETHICS

We, the members of the American Bus Association, in carrying out our role of providing service to the traveling public recognize the need to do so in a professional manner, and to deal with the public and our colleagues with the highest degree of integrity. Therefore, we herewith set forth the following creed which shall govern our endeavors to fulfill our obligations:

1. To adhere to the professional standards of the American Bus Association and to work to further its goals and objectives.

2. To conduct all business affairs with integrity, sincerity, and accuracy in an open and forthright manner.

3. To act with integrity in financial dealing with the public and with entities utilized to help arrange or provide service and accommodations to motorcoach travelers.

4. To conduct our business and operations in a safe manner in order to protect the public and to promote the image of the industry.

5. To work to instill consumer and public confidence in the industry, avoiding any action conducive to discrediting it or membership in the Association.

In addition, we will avoid committing the following acts:

1. Misappropriation of funds deposited with or entrusted to a Member of the Association by another Member or by a person having a business relationship with the bus industry;

2. Willful and wrongful refusal to pay for services rendered by another Member or by a person having a business relationship with

the bus industry, or a willful refusal to make arrangements for payment of such services;

3. Wrongful failure to provide transportation or related services, as promised, and failure to make prompt restitution for any breach of a contractual obligation;

4. Willful violation of Federal or State laws pertaining to the regulation of the intercity bus industry, including rules and regulations promulgated by the U.S. Department of Transportation or applicable country laws, or;

5. Systematic violation of rules, regulations, or policies of the Association.

Source: American Bus Association.

APPENDIX 12:
CONSUMER PROTECTION TIPS FOR CHARTER BUS TRANSPORTATION

1. **How long has the company been in business?** The longer it has offered transportation service the better.

2. **Request the company's U.S. Department of Transportation (USDOT) number that's required for legal operation.** Use the number to check the company's current safety rating.

3. **What is the company's USDOT Safety Rating?** The highest possible rating is "satisfactory." You can find a company's rating from the Federal Motor Carrier Safety Administration (FMCSA) website: [www.safersys.org/CSP_Order.asp]. Search by USDOT number. Never charter from a company with an unsatisfactory rating.

4. **Ask the company to supply a Certificate of Insurance, showing its levels of insurance and effective policy dates.** Accepted levels call for $5 million combined, single-limit liability coverage.

5. **Ask for references.** Never charter from a company not willing to provide references.

6. **What is the size of the company's fleet?** Fleet size provides a gauge to the operator's ability to supply alternate vehicles if needed and insight into the company's success.

7. **Personally inspect the company's office, garage facilities and transportation equipment.** You can tell a lot about a company just by looking.

8. **How old is the equipment?** The newer the equipment (not more than 10 years old), generally means fewer problems.

9. **Is the company a full service company?** Does it have its own maintenance facilities? Can they arrange tours or other special travel services?

10. **For an accurate quote on your trip, provide the company with a detailed itinerary.**

11. **Does your group have special needs, i.e., a video system, beverage galley, disabled access or other equipment?**

12. **Ask if video-equipped equipment is available.** You can view educational video, movies, or sports videos while traveling.

13. **Is the company legally licensed to show motion pictures en route? Only companies licensed by the Motion Picture Association of America may legally show copyrighted movies.** Films rented from a video store are not licensed for public viewing.

14. **Be a smart shopper.** Make sure careful consideration of these consumer tips is balanced against cost. A decision based solely on price may not be the best value.

15. **Ask who pays for the driver's overnight accommodations.** Is it included in the charter cost? Also specify if the driver must stay in the same hotel as your group.

16. **Determine the company's policy for extra mileage costs above the contracted amount.** Find out the company's policy concerning "overage miles" before you select a company, not when you get an inflated bill after you return.

17. **Ask if the company adheres to USDOT driver regulations, which limit the number of hours a driver can work.** A driver is limited to 10 hours of actual driving time. If your itinerary exceeds this limit, how will the company handle your group's needs?

18. **What procedures are followed for on-the-road emergencies?** The company should have access to a nationwide reciprocal maintenance agreement, assuring you of prompt servicing of equipment in all regions of the USA.

19. **Ask if the company has a formal Drug and Alcohol Program.** Specify that the company must supply a copy of their written drug and alcohol policy statement. Never charter transportation from a company that does not strongly enforce a drug- and alcohol-free workplace.

20. **Request a list of current, qualified drivers who have a commercial driver's license, a USDOT driver's file, a current USDOT physical examination and an approved Medical Examiner's Card.**

Source: Trailways Transportation System.

APPENDIX 13:
LIST OF TRAILWAYS TRANSPORTATION MEMBER COMPANIES

A.S. Midway Trailways, Baltimore, MD

Abbott Trailways, Roanoke, VA

Adirondack Trailways, Hurley, NY

Amador Stages Trailways, Sacramento, CA

Amador Trailways of NV, Reno, NV

AmericanStar Trailways, Pismo Beach, CA

Anchor Railways, Whites Creek, TN

Arrow Railways of TX, Killeen, TX

Atlantic Coast Railways, Hagerstown, MD

Burlington Trailways, West Burlington, IA

Capital Trailways of AL, Montgomery, AL

Capital Trailways of Huntsville, Madison, AL

Capital Trailways of MS, Richland, MS

Capitol Trailways of PA, Harrisburg, PA

Cavalier Coach Trailways, Boston, MA

Central States Trailways, Hazelwood, MO

Colonial Trailways, Mobile, AL

Cross Country Tours Trailways, Spartanburg, SC

Dakota Trailways, Spearfish, SD

Dean Trailways of MI, Lansing, MI

Dixon Meyers Trailways, Rochelle, IL

Eagle Trailways of TX, Irving, TX

El Camino Trailways - Reno/Tahoe, Mound House, NV

El Camino Trailways of CA, South San Francisco, CA

Elbow Trailways, Hein-Holland, The Netherlands

Endeavor Trailways, Miami, FL

Excursions Trailways of IN, Ft. Wayne, IN

Excursions Trailways of OH, Ottawa, OH

First Class Trailways, St. Petersburg, FL

First Priority Trailways, District Heights, MD

Flagship Trailways, Cranston, RI

Burlington Trailways, Clearfield, PA

Gentry Trailways, Knoxville, TN

Gold Line Trailways, Tuxedo, MD

Got to Go Trailways, Fort Worth, TX

Great Canadian Trailways, Kitchener, ON, Canada

Heartland Trailways, St. Joseph, MO

Husky Trailways, Festus, MO

King Ward Trailways, Chicopee, MA

Cousin Trailways, Kaukauna, WI

Lakefront Trailways, Cleveland, OH

Lancaster Trailways of Charleston, SC

Lancaster Trailways, the Carolinas, Lancaster, SC

Lion Trailways, Levittown, PA

Lone Star Trailways, Tyler, TX

Louisiana Trailways, Marrero, LA

Martz Trailways, Wilkes-Barre, PA

Memphis Trailways, Memphis, TN

Miller Trailways of IN, Indianapolis, IN

Miller Trailways of KY, Louisville, KY

Myers Trailways, Export, PA

National Coach Trailways, Fredericksburg, VA

New York Trailways, Hurley, NY

Northeast Trailways of ME, Lewiston, ME

Northwestern Trailways, Spokane, WA

Orange Belt Trailways, Visalia, CA

Pacific Coachways Trailways, Garden Grove, CA

Paradise Trailways, Hicksville, NY

Pine Hill Trailways, Hurley, NY

Prairie Coach Trailways, Dell Rapids, SD

Prairie Trailways, Chicago, IL

Rimrock Trailways, Billings, MT

Royal Tours Trailways, Asheboro, NC

Salter Trailways, Jonesboro, LA

Samson Trailways, Atlanta, GA

San Antonio Trailways, San Antonio, TX

Seitz Risen Trailways of Germany, Ruhmansfelden, Bayern/Regen, Germany

Sierra Trailways of TX, South Houston, TX

Silver State Trailways of CA, Placentia, CA

Silver State Trailways of NV, Las Vegas, NV

St. Cloud Trailways, St. Cloud, MN

Starkville Trailways, Ridgeland, MS

Sun Travel Trailways, Beaumont, TX

Susquehanna Trailways, Avis, PA

Swept Away Trailways, Savannah, GA

Thrasher Brothers Trailways, Birmingham, AL

Utah Trailways, Salt Lake City, UT

VIA Trailways, Tempe, AZ

Viking Trailways, Joplin, MO

West Point Trailways, Vails Gate, NY

Source: Trailways Transportation System

APPENDIX 14:
DIRECTORY OF INTERNATIONAL CRUISE LINES AND ASSOCIATED SHIPS

CRUISE LINE	ADDRESS/TELEPHONE	ASSOCIATED SHIPS	WEBSITE
Aida Cruises	Am Strande 3 d Rostock, Germany 18055 Tel: 4903814449301	AIDAura AIDAdiva AIDABella	www.aida.de
American Canadian Caribbean Line, Inc.	461 Water St. P.O. Box 368 Warren, RI 02855 USA Tel: 401-247-0955	Niagara Prince Grande Mariner Grande Caribe	www.accl-smallships.com
American Safari Cruises	3826 18th Ave. W Seattle, WA 98119, USA Tel: 425-776-4700	Safari Quest	www.amsafari.com
Carnival Cruise Lines, Inc.	3655 N.W. 87th Street Miami, FL 33178 USA Tel: 305-599-2600	Holiday Ecstasy	www.carnival.com

CRUISE LINE	ADDRESS/TELEPHONE	ASSOCIATED SHIPS	WEBSITE
Celebrity Cruises	1050 Caribbean Way Miami, FL 33132 USA Tel: 305-982-2727	Sensation Fascination Imagination Inspiration Carnival Destiny Elation Paradise Carnival Victory Carnival Triumph Carnival Glory Carnival Spirit Carnival Pride Carnival Legend Carnival Valor Fantasy Carnival Conquest Carnival Freedom Celebrity Century Celebrity Galaxy Celebrity Mercury Celebrity Infinity Celebrity Summit Celebrity Constellation Celebrity Millennium Celebrity Journey Celebrity Solstice	www.celebrity.com
Classic Cruises of Newport	Christie's Landing Newport, RI 02840 USA Tel: 401-849-3033	Arabella	www.cruisearabella.com

CRUISE LINE	ADDRESS/TELEPHONE	ASSOCIATED SHIPS	WEBSITE
Costa Cruises	Costa Crociere S.P.A. Via XII Ottobre n. 2 Genova, Italy 16121 Tel: +39 (010) 548-3753	Costa Allegra Costa Atlantica Costa Fortuna Costa Mediterranea Costa Magica Costa Concordia	www.costa.it
Crystal Cruises, Inc.	2049 Century Park East Suite 1400 Los Angeles, CA 90067 USA Tel: 310-785-9300	Crystal Symphony Crystal Serenity	www.crystalcruises.com
Cunard Line	6100 Blue Lagoon Dr. Suite 400 Miami, FL 33126 USA Tel: 305-463-3856	Queen Elizabeth 2 Queen Mary 2 Queen Victoria	www.cunardline.com
Discovery Cruise Line	4770 Biscayne Blvd. Penthouse A Miami, FL 33137 USA Tel: 305-704-0904	Discovery Sun	www.discoverycruiseline.com
Discovery World Cruises	1800 S.E. 10th Ave. Suite 205 Fort Lauderdale, FL 33316 USA TEL: 954-623-2689	MV Discovery	www.discoveryworldcruises.com
Disney Cruise Lines	P.O. Box 10210 Lake Buena Vista, FL 32830 USA Tel: 407-566-3589	Disney Magic Disney Wonder	www.disneycruise.disney.go.com

CRUISE LINE	ADDRESS/TELEPHONE	ASSOCIATED SHIPS	WEBSITE
Fred Olsen Cruise Line	White House Road Ipswich Suffolk, UK IP1 5LL Tel: None Listed	Black Watch Braemar Balmoral	None Listed
Hapag Lloyd Kreuzfahrten Gmbh	Ballindamm 25 D-2005 Hamburg, Germany 22095 Tel: 49042135000	Hanseatic Bremen C. Columbus Europa	www.hlkf.de
Holland America Line	300 Elliot Avenue West Seattle, WA 98119 USA Tel: 206-286-3455	Statendam Oosterdam Maasdam Ryndam Veendam Zaandam Rotterdam Volendam Zuiderdam Amsterdam Prinsendam Westerdam Noordam	www.hollandamerica.com
Hotel Playaventura S.I./ Vistamar Canarias S.L.	Office of Almeria Hotel Playadventura S.L. 04740 Roquetas De Mar Almeria, Spain 04740 Tel: 34 950 62 71 53	Vistamar	None Listed
Imperial Majesty Cruise Line	4161 NW 5th Street Suite 200 Plantation, FL 33317 USA Tel: 954-453-4625	Regal Empress	www.imperialmajesty.com

CRUISE LINE	ADDRESS/TELEPHONE	ASSOCIATED SHIPS	WEBSITE
Japan Cruise Line, Inc.	2-5-25 Umeda Kita-ku Head Office Herbis Osaka 15F Osaka, Japan 530-0001 Tel: 06 6347 1496	Pacific Venus	www.venus-cruise.com.jp
Kyma Ship Management, Inc.	1015 North America Way Miami, FL 33132 USA Tel: 305-376-8615	TSS Topaz Mona Lisa	None Listed
Lindblad Expeditions	1415 Westin Ave. Suite 700 Seattle, WA 98101 USA Tel: 206-582-9593	Sea Lion Sea Bird National Geographic Explorer	www.expeditions.com
Mitsui O.s.k. Passenger Line, Ltd	Sankadio Bldg. 1-9-13 Akasaka Minato-KU, 5th Floor Tokyo, Japan 107-8532 Tel: 03 5114 5230	Nippon Maru Fuji Maru	www.mol.co.jp
MSC Cruises	Corso Italia 214 Piano Di Sorrento Napoli, Italy 80063 Tel: 39 081 5321530	MSC Lirica MSC Opera Armonia Sinfonia MSC Poesia MSC Magnifica	www.mscruises.com
New Sea Escape Cruises, Ltd.	3045 N. Federal Highway Suite #7 Fort Lauderdale, FL 33306 USA Tel: 954-453-3380	Island Adventure	www.seaescape.com

CRUISE LINE	ADDRESS/TELEPHONE	ASSOCIATED SHIPS	WEBSITE
Norwegian Cruise Lines	7665 Corporate Center Dr. Miami, FL 33126 USA Tel: 305-436-4952	Norwegian Wind Norwegian Spirit Norwegian Majesty Norwegian Dream Norwegian Sky Norwegian Star Norwegian Sun Norwegian Dawn Norwegian Jewel Norwegian Pearl Norwegian Gem Pride of Aloha Norwegian Jade	www.ncl.com
NYK Cruises Co.	Yusen Building 3-2 Marunouhi 2-Chome Chiyoda-KU Tokyo, Japan 100-0005 Tel: 81 3 3284 5725 or 5650	Asuka II	www.asukacruise.co.jp
P & O Cruises	Richmond House Terminus Terra Southampton, UK SO14 3PN Tel: 02380525252	Oriana Aurora Oceana Arcadia Artemis Ventura Pacific Sun	www.pocruises.com
Palm Beach Cruises	777 E. Port Road Rivera Beach, FL 33404 USA Tel: 561-227-2613	Palm Beach Princess	www.pbcasino.com

CRUISE LINE	ADDRESS/TELEPHONE	ASSOCIATED SHIPS	WEBSITE
Radisson Seven Seas Cruises	600 Corporate Drive Suite 410 Ft. Lauderdale, FL 33334 USA Tel: 954-776-6123	Seven Seas Navigator	www.rssc.com/home./jsp
Residensea	5200 Blue Lagoon Drive Suite 790 Miami, FL 33126 USA Tel: 305-264-9090	The World	www.residensea.com
Royal Caribbean International	1050 Caribbean Way 5th Floor Miami, FL 33132 USA Tel: 305-539-6883	Sovereign of the Seas Monarch of the Seas Majesty of the Seas Legend of the Seas Splendour of the Seas Grandeur of the Seas Rhapsody of the Seas Enchantment of the Seas Voyager of the Seas Vision of the Seas Explorer of the Seas Brilliance of the Seas Radiance of the Seas Mariner of the Seas Jewel of the Seas Navigator of the Seas Serenade of the Seas Empress of the Seas Freedom of the Seas	www.rccl.com

CRUISE LINE	ADDRESS/TELEPHONE	ASSOCIATED SHIPS	WEBSITE
Seabourn Cruise Line	6100 Blue Lagoon Drive Suite 400 Miami, FL 33126 USA Tel: 305-463-3136	Adventure of the Seas Liberty of the Seas Independence of the Seas Seabourn Pride Seabourn Spirit Seabourn Legend Seabourn Odyssey	www.seabourn.com
Services Et Transports Cruise	P.O. Box 639 24 Avenue du Fontvielle Monaco, France 98013 Tel: 33 2 35 24 72 00/26	Club Med 2	None Listed
Sterling Casino Line	101 George King Boulevard Cape Canaveral, FL 32920 USA Tel: 321-783-2212	None Listed	None Listed
Swan Hellenic Cruises	631 Commack Road Suite 1-A Commack, NY 11724 USA Tel: 631-858-1263	None Listed	www.vships.com
Transocean Tours	Touristik GmbH Slavendamm 22 Bremen, Germany 28195 Tel: 042133360	Astor	www.transocean.de
Travel Dynamics International	132 East 70th Street New York, NY 10021 Tel: 212-517-7555	Orion	www.traveldynamicsinternational.com

CRUISE LINE	ADDRESS/TELEPHONE	ASSOCIATED SHIPS	WEBSITE
Unicom Mgt Services, Ltd	Oasis Center P.O. Box 56674 Corner of Gladstone & Kaaiskakis Streets Limassol, Cyprus 3309 Tel: 357 258 90000	Maxim Gorkiy Albatross	None Listed
Windjammer Barefoot Cruises	1759 Bay Road Miami Beach, FL 33119 USA Tel: 305-534-5426	Legacy	www.windjammer.com

Source: Centers for Disease Control and Prevention (CDC).

GLOSSARY

Accommodation—A term used in the context of public accommodations and facilities in which an individual with a disability may not be excluded, denied services, segregated or otherwise treated differently than other individuals by a public accommodation or commercial facility.

Actual Damages—Actual damages are those damages directly referable to the breach or tortious act, and which can be readily proven to have been sustained, and for which the injured party should be compensated as a matter of right.

Advance Purchase Requirement—The requirement that an airfare must be purchased a certain number of days before flight departure.

Aerial Tramway—An electric system of aerial cables with suspended powerless passenger vehicles that are propelled by separate cables attached to the vehicle suspension system and powered by engines or motors at a central location not on board the vehicle.

Air Carrier—Any citizen of the United States who undertakes, whether directly or indirectly or by a lease or any other arrangement, to engage in air transportation.

Air Carrier Access Act—Statute prohibiting discrimination by air carriers against qualified individuals with physical or mental impairments.

Air Carrier Airport—A public, commercial service airport that enplanes annually 2,500 or more passengers and receives scheduled air service.

Air Mile—A distance of approximately 6076 feet.

Airport Bus—A bus used to transport passengers to, from, and within airports.

Airport Transfer Service—Service to and from the airport and the hotel.

Air/Sea—Refers to a ticket that includes both air and land-based travel arrangements.

Air Transportation—Interstate, overseas, or foreign air transportation, or the transportation of mail by aircraft, as defined in the Federal Aviation Act.

Air Travel Card—A credit card issued by an airline that is used for the purchase of air travel.

Ambulation Aids—Devices that help people walk upright, including canes, crutches, and walkers.

American Civil Liberties Union (ACLU)—A nationwide organization dedicated to the enforcement and preservation of rights and civil liberties guaranteed by the federal and state constitutions.

Americans with Disabilities Act (ADA)—A federal law which prohibits discrimination on the basis of a "qualified" disability as set forth in the statute.

Americans with Disability Act Accessibility Guidelines (ADAAG)—Technical standard for accessible design of new construction or alterations adopted by the Department of Justice for places of public accommodation pursuant to Title III of the ADA.

Architectural Barrier—A physical feature of a public accommodation that limits or prevents disabled persons from obtaining the goods or services offered.

Architectural Barriers Act (ABA)—A federal law requiring that buildings and facilities that are designed, constructed or altered with federal funds, or leased by a federal agency, must comply with federal standards for physical accessibility by the disabled.

Baggage—Property a passenger takes with him or her for personal use or convenience.

Baggage Allowance—The size or weight of baggage that a passenger may take on an airline flight without any additional charge.

Base Fare—The price of an airline ticket, before taxes, surcharges and fees are added.

Berth—The bed in the cabin of a ship.

Blackout Dates—The dates on which travel is not available.

Bumping—The airline practice of denying boarding to confirmed ticket holders for a specific flight because the flight was oversold.

Burden of Proof—The duty of a party to substantiate an allegation or issue to convince the trier of fact as to the truth of their claim.

Bus—A passenger-carrying vehicle, powered by diesel, gasoline, battery or alternative fuel engines, used in a common carrier's authorized operations.

Bus Stop—A designated place where a public transport bus stops for the purpose of allowing passengers to board or leave a bus.

Bus Rapid Transit (BRT)—A type of limited-stop service that relies on technology to help speed up the service and operates on exclusive transitways, high-occupancy-vehicle (HOV) lanes, expressways, or ordinary streets.

Cabin—Refers to the passenger area on an airplane or the stateroom on a cruise ship.

Cancellation Fee—A monetary penalty assessed when a passenger cancels their travel plans.

Carrier—A company that transports passengers or freight.

Carry-On Luggage—Refers to luggage that a passenger brings on an airplane and stores in a compartment within the cabin, and which must comply with size limitations.

Coach—Refers to the economy seats on an airplane.

Commuter Rail Service—Also known as metropolitan rail, regional rail or suburban rail, refers to an electric or diesel propelled railway for urban passenger train service consisting of local short distance travel operating between a central city and adjacent suburbs.

Confirmed Reserved Space—Space on a specific date and on a specific flight and class of service of a carrier which has been requested by a passenger, and which the carrier or its agent has verified as being reserved for the accommodation of the passenger.

Connecting Flight—Refers to a change of aircraft for a segment of an airline flight.

Court—The branch of government responsible for the resolution of disputes arising under the laws of the government.

Damages—In general, damages refers to monetary compensation which the law awards to one who has been injured by the actions of another, such as in the case of tortious conduct or breach of contractual obligations.

Debark—To exit an airplane or cruise ship.

Direct Flight—A flight that does not require a change of aircraft, but which may include stops on the way to the destination.

Disability—Under the ADA, an individual is considered disabled if he or she (i) is substantially impaired with respect to a major life activity; (ii) has a record of such an impairment; or (iii) is regarded as having an impairment.

Domestic Fare—A fare charged for travel within a country.

DOT—United States Department of Transportation.

Double Decked Bus—Refers to a high-capacity bus having two levels of seating connected by one or more stairways.

Duty-Free—Items that are exempt from import tax.

Embark—To board an airplane or cruise ship.

Equal Access—Equal opportunity of a qualified person with a disability to participate in or benefit from educational aids, benefits, or services.

ETA—Estimated time of arrival.

ETD—Estimated time of departure.

Express Bus Service—Generally refers to buses that speed up longer trips by operating long distances without stopping.

Express Ferryboat Service—Refers to ferryboat service that operate in peak-hours bypassing intervening islands or that operate high-speed or passenger-only ferries.

Express Rail Service—Generally refers to trains that speed up longer trips by operating long distances without stopping.

FAA—The Federal Aviation Administration.

Facility—Any structure provided by or for a carrier at or near which the carrier picks up or discharges passengers.

Ferryboat—A transit mode comprised of steam or diesel-powered vessels that carry passengers and/or vehicles over a body of water.

First Class—Refers to upgraded seats on an airplane that are more expensive and include certain amenities, such as more space and better meals.

Force Majeure—An event that cannot be reasonably anticipated.

Heavy Rail Service—Also known as metro, subway, rapid transit or rapid rail, refers to an electric railway with the capacity for a heavy volume of traffic, characterized by high speed and rapid acceleration passenger rail cars operating singly or in multi-car trains on fixed rails.

Hub—An airport in which many flights arrive and depart.

Indirect Air Carrier—A person not directly involved in the operation of an aircraft who sells air transportation services to the general public other than as an authorized agent of an air carrier.

Inside Cabin—A stateroom on a cruise ship that has no portholes.

Intercity Bus—Refers to a bus that has a front door only, separate luggage compartments, and usually restroom facilities and high-backed seats for use in high-speed long-distance service.

Jitney—A transit mode comprised of passenger cars or vans operating on fixed routes as demand warrants without fixed schedules or fixed stops.

Judge—The individual who presides over a court, and whose function it is to determine controversies.

Knot—A nautical measure of speed.

Layover—A period of time spent during a trip while waiting for a connecting flight.

Light Rail Service—Also known as a **streetcar, tramway,** or **trolley,** refers to lightweight passenger rail cars operating singly, or in short two-car trains, on fixed rails in right-of-way that is not separated from other traffic for much of the way.

Limited Stop Bus Service—A hybrid between local and express bus service where the stops may be several blocks to a mile or more apart to speed up the trip.

Limited Stop Rail Service—A hybrid between local and express rail service where not all stations and stops are serviced.

Local Bus Service—Generally refers to buses that stop every block or two along a route several miles long.

Local Ferryboat Service—Refers to ferryboats that operate non-stop over short distances.

Local Rail Service—Generally refers to trains that stop at every station on a route.

Mode—A system for carrying transit passengers.

Non-Refundable Fare—A fare that cannot be refunded.

Non-Stop Flight—An airline flight that goes directly to the destination with no intermediate stops.

Non-Transferable Ticket—A ticket that cannot be used by anyone but the person to whom it was issued.

NTSB—The National Transportation Safety Board.

Off-Peak—A period of time when there is less travel and lower fares.

Outside Cabin—A stateroom on a cruise ship that has a porthole.

Overbooking—The practice of selling more seats than are available on an airline flight.

Port—The location where a cruise ship docks.

Public Entities—For the purposes of Title II coverage under the ADA, refers to state and local governments, their departments, agencies or other instrumentalities.

Red Eye—Refers to an overnight airline flight that generally arrives at its destination in the early morning.

Round Trip Ticket—Refers to a flight that includes a return ticket from the destination.

Saturday Night Stay—The requirement that a traveler's trip include a Saturday stay in order to qualify for the lowest fare.

Scheduled Air Service—Any flight scheduled in the current edition of the Official Airline Guide, the air carrier's published schedule, or the computer reservation system used by the air carrier.

School Bus—A bus used to transport children to and from school, as well as for trips, special events and athletic competitions.

Service—Passenger transportation between authorized points or over authorized routes.

Service Animal—Refers to an animal, such as a guide dog, which has been trained to provide assistance to disabled individuals.

Sleeper—The sleeping compartment on a train.

Stateroom—The cabin on a cruise ship.

Station—A facility, other than a terminal, operated by or for a carrier to accommodate passengers.

Statute of Limitations—Any law that fixes the time within which parties must take judicial action to enforce rights or thereafter be barred from enforcing them.

Stopover—A deliberate interruption of a journey at a point between the place of departure and the final destination.

Suburban Bus—Refers to a bus that has front doors only, normally high-backed seats, but no luggage compartments or restroom facilities for use in longer-distance service with relatively few stops.

Terminal—A facility operated or used by a carrier, chiefly to furnish passengers transportation services and accommodations.

Tour—A trip taken by a group of people who travel together and follow a predetermined itinerary.

Tour Bus Service—Bus service designed to take passengers on sight-seeing expeditions around tourist destinations.

Transit Bus—A bus used for public transportation purposes, also referred to as a commuter or city bus.

Travel Advisory—A warning to travelers issued by the Department of State concerning dangerous situations abroad, such as war, natural disaster, etc.

Trip Cancellation Insurance—A type of insurance that provides for a refund if the traveler has to cancel his or her trip after having paid for the trip.

Trolley—A rubber-tired electrically powered passenger vehicle that draws power from overhead lines.

Uniform Federal Accessibility Standard (UFAS)—Technical standard for accessible design of new construction and alterations pursuant to the Architectural Barriers Act.

Unrestricted Fare—An airfare that has no restrictions, such as a black out period or a Saturday stay requirement.

U.S. Equal Employment Opportunity Commission (EEOC)—Federal agency responsible for issuing regulations to enforce the provisions of Title I of the ADA.

Van—A vehicle having a typical seating capacity of 5 to 15 passengers and classified as a van by vehicle manufacturers.

Water Taxis—Very small passenger-only ferries that operate in both fixed-route and on-demand service, depending on the time of day and patronage levels.

BIBLIOGRAPHY AND ADDITIONAL RESOURCES

American Bus Association (Date Visited: September 2008) http://www.buses.org/

American Public Transportation Association (Date Visited: September 2008) http://www.apta.com/

Amtrak (Date Visited: September 2008) http://www.amtrak.com/

Black's Law Dictionary, Fifth Edition. St. Paul, MN: West Publishing Company, 1979.

Centers for Disease Control and Prevention (Date Visited: September 2008) http://www.cdc.gov/

Department of Homeland Security, Office for Civil Rights and Civil Liberties (Date Visited: September 2008) http://www.dhs.gov/

Federal Aviation Administration (Date Visited: September 2008) http://www.faa.gov/

Federal Motor Carrier Safety Administration (Date Visited: September 2008) http://www.safersys.org/

Federal Railroad Administration (Date Visited: September 2008) http://www.fra.dot.gov/

Greyhound Lines, Inc. (Date Visited: September 2008) http://www.greyhound.com/

NationMaster (Date Visited: September 2008) http://www.nationmaster.com/

Office of Aviation Enforcement and Proceedings, Aviation Consumer Protection Division (Date Visited: September 2008) http://airconsumer.ost.dot.gov/

School Bus Information Clearinghouse (Date Visited: September 2008) http://sbi.elitedecision.com/

The U.S. Department of Justice (Date Visited: September 2008) http://www.usdoj.gov/

The U.S. Department of Transportation (Date Visited: September 2008) http://www.dot.gov/

The U.S. Equal Opportunity Commission (Date Visited: September 2008) http://www.eeoc.gov/

Trailways Transportation System (Date Visited: September 2008) http://www.trailways.com/

Transportation Security Administration (Date Visited: September 2008) http://www.tsa.gov/

Vessel Sanitation Program (Date Visited: September 2008) http://www.cdc.gov/nceh/vsp/